Praise for FT Guide to Busin‹

'Despite years of sales and training experience, w̲ Networking I found it really hard to do. Over t learnt a lot about networking; then I read this excellent, highly practical book, only to find out so much more about business networking. It is written in an easy to read, down to earth style that makes it simple to learn lessons (and there are loads of them). Even if you are an experienced networker (combining online and offline), I highly recommend you read this book.

If you are new to networking, nervous about or not getting enough results from your networking – you definitely need to buy this book.'

Jon Baker – Business Coach with Venture-now

'If you ever thought face to face or social networking was difficult or would not work for you – think again! This book makes it easy and really shows why networking online and offline should be your first choice in how to do more business, more enjoyably than ever before. It should be your networking Bible!'

Bruce King – Author of How To Double Your Sales

'If you want to achieve workplace success, and build a strong personal brand, then business networking is critical. Take the first step to understanding and implementing networking strategies by reading Heather's book!'

Dan Schawbel, author of Me 2.0 and founder of Millennial Branding, LLC

'A great practical guide to all aspects of networking – stuffed with lots of quick and easy tips to help you leverage the power of your network.'

Ivan Misner, NY Times Bestselling Author and Founder of BNI and Referral Institute

'If business networking was an applied science, Heather Townsend's book would be the curriculum, survival guide and roadmap to this often misunderstood aspect of life and business. Having studied and interviewed the UK and the world's top thought leaders on the subject, coupled with her own practical experience, this book offers an objective overview, discussing business networking's global principles which are clearly laid out and explained.

Whether it be face-to-face, or making connections through Twitter, every aspect of connecting with others is uncovered and explained. Readers can hope to have a shifted perception about how they should view networking but most importantly, to learn how to stop wasting time and invest in the actions which, further down the line, will lead to personal referrals or valuable connections – the end goal. This guide should be read by entrepreneurs, job seekers, employees at all levels, and, in my opinion, high school kids ready to take on the world. Nothing evangelical, easy-to-read, practical and highly recommended.'

David Stoch, Director, Meerkat PR

'There are few people as proficient as Heather in both face-to-face and online networking. Queen of Twitter and founder of the impressive Executive Village network, she shares her knowledge in a very practical way in this really valuable handbook. It will give you the confidence and tools you need to excel in both worlds, joining up your on- and offline activity for networking success. I'd recommend this book to anyone in business – whether you are looking to build a company or boost your professional career.'

Sonja Jefferson, Director of Valuable Content

'Heather delivers the ultimate guide for the ultimate business tool of the 21st Century.

Business networking is, in the 2010s, what talent management was during the 2000s. It is the essence of sustainable competitive advantage for business. As "talent management" was deemed by some, to their detriment, to be a load of "mumbo jumbo" nonsense, the same can be said of attitudes to networking. Networking is one of those areas where you need to ask yourself "Can you afford not to?" rather than "Can I spare the time for this?"

Heather's guide to Networking covers all the "etiquette" that enables people to develop into effective networkers, whilst not being so prescriptive that it stifles individuality. The guide covers all the different "media" by which networking can take place. A guide for those new to networking, as well as those "older heads" that need to re-evaluate or refine their approach.

A must read.'

Marc Lawn, Founder of The Business GP

'More so now than ever it is crucial for all business professionals to actively develop and grow their networks daily. Through sharing stories of real life successes, Heather brings the art of joined up networking to life.

The many tips, activities and suggestions aid both novice and expert networkers alike to create a bespoke strategy for business networking; developing an individually tailored approach that uses a wide variety of traditional methods and modern media that is right for them.

Acting on the tried and tested FITTER™ approach gives you both jam for today and more importantly helps you build a network that will provide jam for tomorrow.

Since reading this book, I can genuinely say I have come away fired up to build on already strong network to get them to deliver more results for me!'

Karen Spillane, Learning & Development Professional

The Financial Times Guide to Business Networking

FT Prentice Hall
FINANCIAL TIMES

In an increasingly competitive world, we believe it's quality of thinking that gives you the edge – an idea that opens new doors, a technique that solves a problem, or an insight that simply makes sense of it all. The more you know, the smarter and faster you can go.

That's why we work with the best minds in business and finance to bring cutting-edge thinking and best learning practice to a global market.

Under a range of leading imprints, including *Financial Times Prentice Hall*, we create world-class print publications and electronic products bringing our readers knowledge, skills and understanding, which can be applied whether studying or at work.

To find out more about Pearson Education publications, or tell us about the books you'd like to find, you can visit us at **www.pearsoned.co.uk**

PEARSON

The Financial Times Guide to Business Networking

How to use the power of online and offline networking for business success

Heather Townsend

**Financial Times
Prentice Hall
is an imprint of**

Harlow, England • London • New York • Boston • San Francisco • Toronto • Sydney • Singapore • Hong Kong
Tokyo • Seoul • Taipei • New Delhi • Cape Town • Madrid • Mexico City • Amsterdam • Munich • Paris • Milan

Pearson Education Limited

Edinburgh Gate
Harlow CM20 2JE
Tel: +44 (0)1279 623623
Fax: +44 (0)1279 431059
Website: www.pearsoned.co.uk

First published in Great Britain in 2011

© Heather Townsend 2011

The right of Heather Townsend to be identified as author of this work has been
asserted by her in accordance with the Copyright, Designs and Patents Act 1988.

Pearson Education is not responsible for the content of third party internet sites.

ISBN: 978-0-273-74582-2

British Library Cataloguing-in-Publication Data
A catalogue record for this book is available from the British Library

Library of Congress Cataloging-in-Publication Data
Townsend, Heather.
   The Financial times guide to business networking : how to use the power of online and
offline networking for business success / Heather Townsend.
     p.cm.
   Includes index.
   ISBN 978-0-273-74582-2 (pbk.)
   1. Business networks. I. Title.
   HD69.S8T69 2011
   650.1'3--dc22
                                        2011014895

Microsoft screenshots reprinted with permission from Microsoft Corporation.

10 9 8 7 6 5 4 3 2 1
15 14 13 12 11

Typeset in 9pt Stone Serif by 3
Printed by Ashford Colour Press Ltd., Gosport

Contents

Acknowledgements

There are many people to whom I owe a sincere debt of gratitude – without them, this book never would have been started, written or finished to such a high standard.

Without the inspiration and suggestions of Mariam Cook and Bryony Thomas this book would still be in my head rather than on paper.

There are two people who have been by my side through my journey to get published and write this book. The suggestions, combined expertise and continual faith of Sonja Jefferson and Robert Watson have helped me craft a book that people want to read. I'm not sure whether I have ever told the two of you, but I never would have got this far or this fast without your help. For that I will forever be in your debt.

Writing a book while growing and running a business is not easy. I've been able to do both only with the help and support of my great team, Jon Baker and Helen Stothard. Without your occasional pep talks, 'gentle' nagging, diary management, guidance, belief in me, daily support and championing of what I wanted to do, I never would have finished the book.

Then there are all the people who kindly gave up their time to be interviewed for this book, whose collective experiences and stories helped shape my own thinking and ideas: Ivan Misner, Guy Clapperton, Brad Burton, Andy Lopata, Dan Schwabel, Brian Inksters, Hamish Taylor, Mike Briercliffe, Anthony Lloyd, Gary Ives, Jon Shaw, Jonathan Senior, Neil Ryder, Bryony Thomas, Mariam Cook, Melissa Kidd, Karen Spillane, Gina Wadsworth, Eli Barbary, Maggie Langley, Autumn St John, Jeremy Marchant, Alicia Cowan, Wendy Johnson, Sharon Gaskin, Lisa Williams, Elaine Clark, Maxine Welford, Lisa Garwood and Babs Morse.

And finally, there are three people who are the reason I get up in the morning (often far earlier than I would like!). I just want for them to be as proud of me as I am of them and to return my unconditional love.

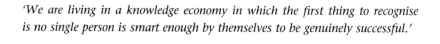

'We are living in a knowledge economy in which the first thing to recognise is no single person is smart enough by themselves to be genuinely successful.'

Hamish Taylor, Shinergise Partners Ltd, www.shinergise.com

Introduction

The phone rang late on a snowy Friday afternoon just before the start of the Christmas holidays. It was Lee Duncan, a member of my virtual mastermind group, with some work for me from one of his contacts, to run a social media workshop in January. Was this luck? Serendipity? Far from it. This phone call was proof that the best way to advance your career and business is via networking.

My interest in joined up networking – the art of combining face-to-face networking with online networking – started when I found myself at the wrong end of a corporate downsizing. My in-house network suddenly vanished and I had to create a new network in a world of strangers. Early into my life as a business owner, I quickly found that the easy way to generate work for myself was via the people I knew. With a very young family, and client work which could take me away for days at a time, I turned to online networking to supplement my face-to-face networking efforts. It was this winning combination of face-to-face and online networking which enabled me to singlehandedly build a business which, within two years, generated an annual income significantly greater than my previous salary. My network, and my continual focus on networking activities, is the reason why my business has sky rocketed and become one of the 30 per cent of all start-up businesses which are still trading two years on. It's also the reason I was approached to write this book.

I am not an isolated example – for a professional, networking is the fastest and most effective way to build a business or career. Professionals report that 80 per cent of their business comes from people they know. They know that networking, done correctly, will increase your pool of contacts, build awareness of what you do, and motivate those valuable referrals and identify career-enhancing job openings. If you network effectively, the relationships you create will generate a stream of opportunities from which you can choose. As you will discover in this book, many successful professionals generate all their business through networking activity alone.

In the past, networking was an activity conducted face-to-face: through formal and informal groups such as professional associations, networking clubs, breakfast meetings and events. These remain important today, but with the meteoric rise of online forums and social networking sites, networking on the web has now really come into its own. Sites such as LinkedIn, Facebook and Twitter enable busy professionals to manage networks of contacts many times larger than is possible face-to-face and to generate consistent opportunities without even leaving their desks. This book will show you how to build a successful joined up networking strategy, which will allow you to pick the most effective mix of networking activities for you.

During the past ten years, I have trained and coached more than 1000 professionals at every level of a business. As a result, I've observed first hand that networking is a core competency that any business professional must master, whether you are looking to move up the career ladder internally or set up and grow your own practice or business. There are thousands of books and training resources on how to conduct yourself when networking face-to-face; there are a growing number of commentators on how to get the best out of networking online. Until this book there has been no single resource for professionals on what is needed to excel in both arenas and how to join up your networking efforts, saving time and generating results more easily for greater business and career success.

Who is this book for?

This book is written for professionals – lawyers, bankers, accountants, coaches, trainers, advisors and consultants: experts in their field with specialist skills, typically for hire. It focuses on the unique needs of this sector. Regardless of whether you sell your time for money, your time really does equate to money. For this reason you have to constantly balance working for your clients and marketing your services to get more clients. In this book you will find practical guidance to help you network efficiently so that you can maximise your productive time and deliver exceptional service and results. Networking is an immensely valuable but time-consuming tool. As Rob Brown, author of *How To Build Your Reputation*,[1] said: 'You don't get paid for networking, you get paid on the results of your networking.' Joining up and integrating your online and offline activities will get you better results for far less effort.

[1] Brown, R., *How To Build Your Reputation: The secrets of becoming the 'go to' professional in a crowded marketplace*, Ecademy Press, 2007.

Most professionals know that effective networking is vital if they want to be successful in what they do. Some may have years of experience of networking in person but be daunted by the world of online networking. Others are a whiz at social networking on the web but enter any face-to-face networking event with extreme trepidation. Many professionals don't network well at all. This is dangerous: get it wrong and at best you'll lose out on opportunities; at worst you can severely damage your professional credibility.

This book teaches you the skills you need to avoid the pitfalls and excel at networking both online and face-to-face. It will help you feel equally comfortable when building business relationships face-to-face or via social networking, and help you use your time efficiently and get best results by combining the two.

For those who network well, the rewards are huge: get your personal contacts to do your marketing for you and you won't need to worry about where the next client or job is coming from – you can pick and choose your ideal assignments and focus on delivering the best service to your clients.

How to use this book

This book is written so you can either read from cover to cover or dip in and out.

At the end of each chapter are:

■ exercises for you to do to put into practice what you have just learned

■ links and references to further resources.

The book is split into four discrete parts.

Part 1 The joined up approach to business networking

Part 1 concentrates on the thinking behind a successful approach to business networking. In this section we explore:

■ what networking is and isn't

■ the four ingredients needed for a successful joined up networking strategy

■ the behaviours and attitudes of great networkers.

Part 2 Online and face-to-face networking options explored

Part 2 identifies all the different types of networking available today and how to maximise your effectiveness with each type. In this part you will discover:

- where and when you should network online or in person
- how to make best use of your time when networking regardless of where you are networking
- the pros and cons of each different type of networking
- how to use your blog to increase the impact of your networking.

Part 3 Essential networking skills for the joined up networker

Part 3 helps you acquire the necessary skills to excel as a networker. You will find out how to:

- make a great first impression with everyone you meet
- effectively work a room
- create a connection and start a positive relationship with everyone you meet – regardless of where you meet them or their cultural background
- turn your network into your own online community
- use a checklist to help you network efficiently.

Part 4 Putting your joined up approach to networking into action

Part 4 brings together everything you have learned and prompts you to devise your own successful joined up networking strategy and plan. You will learn how to:

- set your own networking goals to generate the business and career success you need
- measure the progress you are making with your networking activities
- decide who you need to recruit into your network
- make the most of the time and resources you have available to network.

At the end of the book you will find a section on additional resources to help you continue your networking journey, such as:

- suggested books and blogs on different aspects of networking
- contact details for networking groups
- instructions to download worksheets and templates referenced in this book.

And finally

Come and have a chat with me on Twitter, @heathertowns, or drop me a line at heather@theefficiencycoach.co.uk. I'd love to hear your networking success stories and will publish the best on www.joinedupnetworking.com – my blog site on networking.

The joined up approach to business networking

If I say networking to you, what do you think about? I would hazard a guess that most of you will have thought about a group of strangers in a room talking to each other.

Is this what we really mean by business or professional networking?

Part 1 of this book will first dispel this commonly held view that networking is all about talking to strangers at an event, and define for you what networking is and isn't. It will then dig deeper into the four ingredients needed for your joined up networking to be successful. Then finally, we look at the behaviours and attitudes that define the great networkers.

1

Why network?

What topics are covered in this chapter?

- How networking can positively benefit your business and career

- Why networking is misunderstood or avoided

- What networking is and what it is not

- Why invest time in building your network now, and how much time it will take

- The powerful benefits of including online and face-to-face networking in your networking strategy

- How the skills and tools for both types of networking are complementary

- When to use online or face-to-face networking

By the end of this first chapter you'll understand why networking is such a useful tool for professionals today and the opportunity it presents if you get it right. You'll learn why many people get it wrong or avoid it. We'll introduce you to face-to-face and online networking and why a networking strategy that combines the two will get you the best results.

'You are now competing with everyone on a global scale. There is no job security at all, and now it is all about being found instead of submitting your resume. Networking is the way to be found, and how the smart people get jobs and opportunities now. That is the big difference from even five years ago.'

Dan Schawbel, author of Me 2.0: Build a powerful brand to achieve career success[1]

---

[1] Schawbel, D., *Me 2.0: Build a powerful brand to achieve career success*, Kaplan Trade, 2010.

Whether you are advancing your career or developing your own business, networking is *the* most effective way to build awareness, get found and generate opportunities. Go and sit in a café near your work at lunchtime and tune into the chatter around you – chances are you'll overhear a conversation that goes something like this:

'You are thinking of re-doing your website/contacting a recruitment consultant/changing accountants? The person you should be talking to is X.'

Through effective networking activity *you* can become the known and recommended expert in your field. And the power of recommendation is extremely strong. Most high-value purchases, such as hiring a new employee or engaging a new supplier, involve an element of risk. It's this risk which is why someone will always place more faith and trust in a recommendation rather than someone unknown to them or their network.

Get your networking right and others will do the job of selling for you, spreading the word about your services, products or skills – your own sales force happy to spot opportunities on your behalf, and for free!

'Our networking activities, led to our profit and turnover doubling every year for the last four years, even through the credit crunch and recession.'
Gina Wadsworth, partner in Contact Consultants[2] and director of BNI, the world's largest networking organisation

Effective networking will build your profile, generate genuine opportunities for you – new career opportunities, new partners, new clients. It will extend the strength of the community around you and help you find the answers and tools you need to solve your business problems.

You could have the best product or service out there, or be the most amazing employee to hire, but if no one knows about it or you, how are you going to be found? That's why it is so important for any professional to develop and maintain a strong network of people who can help spread the word about your products, services or skills.

❝Networking has always been a highly effective tool❞

Networking has always been a highly effective tool. As long as commerce has existed, traders have banded together for the common protection against enemies, to govern the conduct of trade and help each other out. Chambers of commerce, which have traditionally provided a hub for networking activities, have been in existence since the 1700s. But in today's global,

---

[2] www.contactconsultants.co.uk

knowledge-based economy, networking has really come to the fore. We have far greater choice and access to people than ever before, but less time or inclination to spend on finding the right person for the job. This is why people are now using their networks more and more, to help them rapidly get to the best solution at the first time of asking. With the rise of online networking via social media you can now build a far larger and more engaged network more easily and more quickly than ever before.

Lack of investment in building a strong network will leave you exposed when you need to find new opportunities – be they a new job or new clients. The most effective way to find a new job or new business is via your network. However, a strong network takes time to build and nurture, and will start to bear fruit only once this is done.

---

case study

Jon Shaw, an IT project manager, needed a new job fast. His soon-to-be ex-employers decided to shut his office, two years earlier than originally planned, in the process making him and many other employees redundant. Jon used LinkedIn to communicate to his network that he was in the market for a new job. One month later, after many phone calls and meetings with his network, a friend recommended Jon for a six-month contract position which hadn't yet been formally advertised. Jon was subsequently hired for the contract position, and after three months in the role was offered the job on a permanent basis.

---

case study

Little did Jeremy Marchant, co-owner at Emotional Intelligence at Work, realise how important his relationship with Dave, a Business Link skills advisor, would actually turn out to be. As a result of the relationship which Jeremy and Dave built up over three lunches, Jeremy has received a steady stream of work from Dave's referrals and recommendations. One of these pieces of work ended up being a lucrative 16-month stress management programme within a local hospital.

Why networking is misunderstood or avoided

Does this sound familiar? Work is a little thin on the ground for your firm, so the edict comes down from on high: *'Everyone needs to get out networking to drum up business.'* Or your manager is telling you: *'You need to get out there and network to improve your profile.'* You've received no training on how to network and suddenly you are required to be out there 'networking'. Whatever that actually means ...

Sadly, this is an all-too-common occurrence in business. Is it any wonder that professionals often hate networking and will go to great lengths to avoid actually having to network, particularly when many organisations expect their staff to network in their own time rather than on company time?

Networking is probably one of the most misunderstood skills today's professionals need for career and business success. It is not:

■ the start of the sales process

■ a cosy chat

■ solely about meeting new people or 'working a room'.

It's these misunderstandings which mean that professionals can 'blunder' into networking, whether face-to-face or online, and due to a lack of skill become ineffective networkers. After a while, most people, when hitting their head against a brick wall, stop. It's the same with networking – if you don't get any results in the short or medium term, you will quickly become disheartened with networking and give up.

This lack of networking ability causes many professionals to stop networking. How much easier is it to meet new people if you know how to start a conversation or relate to anyone you meet? How less scary is a room full of people talking if you know how to break into and out of groups? How much nicer is everyone you meet when you are not trying to sell them something?

'To stand up for the first time in a networking meeting and talk about my business for 60 seconds was the most terrifying thing of my entire life.'
Gina Wadsworth, partner at Contact Consultants and BNI director

Many businesses, often through ignorance or fear, routinely block their employees' access to social networking sites such as Facebook, LinkedIn and Twitter. These are all fantastic online networking tools, which, as I've found for my business and career, are essential tools for today's savvy networkers. Even among those professionals who can access online networking sites at work, many don't know how or where to start with online networking or struggle to gain sufficient momentum to generate results from their time and effort. Consequently, many professionals' efforts at online networking fizzle out after a couple of weeks. For example, a report by Barracuda Labs in December 2009 found that 73 per cent of Twitter user accounts have tweeted less than ten times.[3]

Successful networkers invest time and energy growing and maintaining their network. For example, Karen Spillane, a training professional, spends 30 minutes every day keeping in touch with her network. Many professionals, when faced with chargeable time targets or high levels of client demands, see networking as a luxury rather than a necessity. If you are being measured only on your chargeable time billed, or client satisfaction, what incentive do you have to network?

❝ What incentive do you have to network? ❞

I worked part time for a couple of years after my children were born. I thought my job was pretty secure, I didn't have any business development responsibility, and I was enjoying what I was doing. Why did I need to network? More importantly, between work and family, when did I have time to network? While you may not be a busy working parent, it is a common phenomenon – many professionals don't see a reason to network. They have access to all the answers they need within their current setup, they are not responsible for business development, and they are happy in the job they are in. So, why network? When the recession hit in the UK, many people, including myself, realised that their job wasn't all that secure, and the lack of investment in their network had left them very exposed.

What networking is and what it is not

At its very simplest, networking is about meeting people and interacting with them. Effective business networking is the process of building up mutually beneficial relationships for your career or business.

Professionals fundamentally network for four reasons:

1 Improve their profile, i.e. being 'found'.

2 Generate opportunities such as a new job or new clients.

3 Extend and strengthen the community around them.

4 Find answers and 'tools'.

---

[3] Barracuda Labs 2009 Annual Report, www.BarracudaLabs.com

When you talk about networking, many people connect networking merely with formal networking clubs and associations such as BNI, the world's largest business networking organisation. Without realising it, most of us are consistently networking throughout our waking hours. You may not badge all these activities as networking, but they are all ways in which we network:

- Phoning your mother or a friend for your regular catch-up.
- Writing and posting up a new blog post.
- Introducing yourself to a new member of your club or society.
- Exchanging some pleasantries on a phone call before getting down to business.
- Logging into your Facebook account and reading your friend's status updates.
- Attending a friend's wedding.
- Inviting your work colleagues over for a meal.
- Answering a question posted up on an online forum.
- Regularly attending a business networking club.
- Updating your Twitter account with what you have had for lunch.
- Telling your partner about what happened to you at work today.
- Talking to the person next to you in the queue for the coffee at a conference.
- Going to drinks after work with your team.

What networking is not is *pitching*. Too often people see networking as the start of the sales process, and it is the most common mistake people make when networking. Effective networking is not about selling, it is about developing strong relationships in which work and opportunities will come via, not from! If you are mistakenly selling while out networking, you will be unpopular and damage your credibility.

'People at networking events often don't want to meet lawyers and accountants and network with them, because they tend to get pitched to. This is the reason many professionals sometimes find networking events inhospitable.'

Andy Lopata, co-author of . . . And Death Came Third![4]

---

[4] Lopata, A., *. . . And Death Came Third! The definitive guide to networking and speaking in public*, Book Shaker, 2006.

Why invest time in building your network right now

Many people start to proactively network when they want something, for example a new job or new clients. This is too late. Core to any networker's continual success are strong relationships built on a foundation of trust. These relationships and trust don't magically appear on a first or second meeting; they take time to establish. This means that it is best to build and invest time in your network at least six months before you need to call upon it.

Smart people are using networking to be found and get the best pieces of business and assignments. What are you personally missing out on by not proactively networking?

The time investment needed for networking

'The main problem we all have in business is a lack of time. Time is our most valuable resource. That's why networking is key to success for today's professionals. Successful networkers invest time nurturing and building their network, so their network does most of the work of generating leads, referrals and new business for them.'

Gina Wadsworth, partner at Contact Consultants and BNI director

Networking takes time. You and I both know that time equals money in your world. Effective networking is the most efficient way to generate the results you require for your business and career success. Throughout this book, you will read about how others network effectively, and the resultant time they invest in their networking activities. I am not suggesting as a result of reading this book you copy their example; you need to find the right level of networking for you personally. Let me give you an example. Many people want to know how I manage to generate 80 per cent of my business via my networking activity, basically so that they can replicate my success! When they hear about the time investment taken to do that, they often decide they can't in fact afford to spend the time. At the end of the day, it's all about personal choice. You have a choice about how much time you will spend networking, by what means you will network, and how much success you will generate for yourself when networking.

As you read through this book, I encourage you to think of small things which you could easily add into your day which will make a positive difference to your career or business.

Why include both online and face-to-face networking in your networking strategy

'It's now not about face-to-face networking *or* online networking, it is about *and*.'

Ivan Misner, founder of BNI

In the past five years the tools available to networkers have increased drastically with the arrival of online networking. In the past, networking was an activity conducted face-to-face through formal and informal groups such as professional associations, networking clubs, breakfast meetings and events. Your little black book of contacts, probably still was a black book or Rolodex!

These face-to-face networking events remain important today, but with the meteoric rise of online forums and social networking sites, networking on the web has now come into its own. As global virtual teams become increasingly prevalent, a successful professional has to transcend organisational, cultural, functional and geographical boundaries ... but we can still only be in one physical place at any one time!

Sites and software such as LinkedIn and Twitter enable busy professionals to manage large networks of contacts across cultural, functional and geographical boundaries – many times larger than is possible face-to-face – and to generate consistent opportunities for those professionals prepared to invest time in them.

If you haven't yet added online networking into your networking strategy, one of your competitors definitely is, and they will be generating opportunities which previously may have come your way. For example, Cathy Richardson, a UK-based headhunter who specialises in the automotive industry, uses her LinkedIn network to identify and find potential candidates. When she is looking for suitable candidates she is more likely to contact those with a complete and active LinkedIn profile. Can you or your business afford not to combine online networking with face-to-face networking?

How skills and tools for both types of networking are complementary

'In the new world of social networking, the same rules for face-to-face networking still apply.'

Guy Clapperton, journalist and writer of This Is Social Media: Blog, tweet, link your way to business success'[5]

---

[5] Clapperton, G., *This Is Social Media: Blog, tweet, link your way to business success*, Capstone, 2009.

In reality most face-to-face networking is about people standing around and talking to each other. Online networking is no different. The location may change to an internet forum or social networking site, but it is still people standing around and talking to each other. It's how well you do this 'standing around and talking', whether face-to-face or online, that will determine your success as a networker.

❝Treat people in the online world with courtesy and respect❞

I have found that the skills needed to succeed in online networking are just the same as face-to-face networking – it is still about how you meet, engage and maintain your relationships with people. Treat people in the online world with courtesy and respect, and trust will build within your online relationships in just the same way as if you were meeting them face-to-face.

When to use online or face-to-face networking

Everyone should use a mix of online or face-to-face networking within their networking strategy. (In Part 4 of this book, we show you how to put together your own networking strategy.) However, there will always be times when it is more effective to focus more on one or the other. Let's illustrate this with four examples.

Raj sells high-value and complex legal services. The buyers of his service are normally directors and senior managers within the public sector, who tend not to be regular online networkers. Raj is more likely to meet these people if he focuses more of his time on face-to-face networking rather than online networking. Raj uses his online networking time, mostly on LinkedIn, to stay in touch with his network, but also to find potential suppliers and employees for his business.

Jane is a lawyer who specialises in working with mothers who run their own business, 'mumpreneurs'. As 'mumpreneurs' are heavy users of online networking, Jane focuses the majority of her networking time on Twitter and internet forums aimed at female entrepreneurs. Jane is very selective with her face-to-face networking and spends her face-to-face networking time at conferences aimed at 'mumpreneurs'. She uses her time at the conferences to strengthen her relationships with her online business contacts by spending time with them in person.

Clint wants to re-locate from London to Edinburgh to be closer to his family. He wants a new role within the audit department of a mid-sized accountancy practice. His current practice does not have a presence within Scotland so he is looking for a new employer. He uses LinkedIn to 'meet' auditors and recruitment managers from Edinburgh-based firms. Once he has 'met' a useful contact on LinkedIn, he aims to set up a phone call to get to know them better.

Sarah works for an international management consultancy, at their London headquarters. She is ambitious and wants to make partner within her current firm. She is aware that to achieve her career ambitions and get the right assignments, she needs an extensive network and 'good' profile within the firm. She focuses her networking time, attending internal firm events and volunteering for cross-firm assignments, projects and committees. She uses Facebook to strengthen the relationships she has with the people she works with.

As you can see, there is no one-size-fits-all answer. To decide on the right balance between online and face-to-face networking for your particular business and career goals, you need to ask yourself the following questions:

1   What am I trying to achieve with my networking strategy? New business? New job? New team members? Relationships with new suppliers?

2   Where do people well connected to the people I want to meet (e.g. introducers) spend their time, both physically and virtually?

3   How IT literate are the people well connected to my target market?

4   How much time in my personal and professional life do I have to attend regular face-to-face informal and formal networking events?

5   Where are the people I want to meet located and how easily can I spend time in that location?

6   Do I need to be able to meet people face-to-face before I can achieve my networking objective?

7   How can I use online networking to complement my face-to-face networking?

Summary

Networking is the process by which we choose to meet people and interact with them. Without realising it, most of us are consistently networking throughout our waking hours. Effective business networking is the process of building up mutually beneficial relationships for your career or business.

Professionals fundamentally network for four reasons:

1 Improve their profile, i.e. being 'found'.

2 Generate opportunities such as a new job or new clients.

3 Extend and strengthen the community around them.

4 Find answers and 'tools'.

You have a choice about how much time you will spend networking, by what means you will network, and how much success you will generate for yourself when networking.

Professionals who are keen for career and business success can no longer afford to ignore online networking. Online networking is being used successfully by professionals of all ages and levels of expertise to find new clients and jobs.

In reality, most face-to-face networking is about people standing around and talking to each other. Online networking is no different. It's how well you do this 'standing around and talking', whether face-to-face or online, that will determine your success as a networker.

Use online social networking sites such as Twitter and LinkedIn to widen your reach and keep in contact with a large network. Use face-to-face networking to strengthen and personalise relationships with people important to your career and business.

There is no one-size-fits-all answer for how much online versus face-to-face networking you should do. Only you personally can find the right balance between online and face-to-face networking to help you achieve your personal aims and objectives.

ACTION POINTS

▦ Would you call yourself a proactive or passive networker? What could you start to do to become a proactive networker?

▦ If you are avoiding networking, what's stopping you from networking? How could networking benefit you personally?

▦ What personal goals or objectives do you have which you could use your network to help you achieve?

▦ Find a mentor skilled in both online and face-to-face networking who can help guide you to become a successful networker.

▦ Identify how you can include online networking and face-to-face networking within your networking strategy.

■ Sign up to LinkedIn and join 'The Financial Times Guide to Business Networking' group on LinkedIn.

■ Find someone in your network who is successful at online and/or face-to-face networking and learn how they use online and/or face-to-face networking to help achieve their career and business aims.

■ If you don't enjoy networking, what's stopping you from enjoying it? What could you do to start enjoying networking?

Further resources

Books

Get Off Your Arse, Brad Burton, 4Publishing, 2009.

Professional Networking for Dummies, Donna Fisher, John Wiley & Sons, 2001.

Confident Networking for Career Success and Satisfaction, Gael Lindenfield and Stuart Lindenfield, Piatkus Books, 2005.

Brilliant Networking: What the best networkers, know, do and say, 2nd edition, Stephen D'Souza, Prentice Hall, 2010.

Blogs

Joined Up Business Networking www.joinedupnetworking.com

2

How to create opportunities via networking

What topics are covered in this chapter?

- What are the four ingredients needed to consistently generate opportunities via networking
- How to generate these four ingredients within your networking strategy
- How to calculate your opportunity score

In the last chapter you learned what an effective networking strategy can do for your business and career, particularly if you combine your online and offline activities. As we stated, the skills, behaviours and attitude you need to make it work are complementary in both the virtual and real worlds – the same rules apply. This chapter gives you the four ingredients needed for effective networking activity.

1 Credibility

Before someone is willing to recommend you to someone in their network, they need to know that you are credible and reliable – a trustworthy referral. How do your actions and what you communicate impact on your credibility?

2 Personal brand

Networking is personal – it's about you, your 'brand' and how you communicate your brand to others. How do you present yourself to the world?

If someone Googles your name, what do they find? When they meet you at an event, what do you say?

3 Visibility

With people's networks increasing in size rapidly, how do you get to be that trusted person who your network remembers and introduces to others?

4 Social capital

People help out others in their network because they want to. What do you need to do to get your network to actively help you?

In this chapter we show you a simple way to measure your performance in each of these four ingredients. The rest of the book will show you how to improve your skills and performance in each of these areas to become a successful networker.

The four ingredients needed to consistently generate opportunities via networking

While it is impossible to predict where your next opportunity will come from via your networking activities, it is possible to improve the likelihood of generating opportunities via your network.

The likelihood of opportunities, i.e. referrals and recommendations, which you attract as a networker can be defined by the following equation:

$$Opportunity = Credibility \times (Personal\ brand + Visibility + Social\ capital)$$

where

Opportunity represents an opportunity score – the greater this number, the higher the likelihood of opportunities coming to you.
Credibility = your personal credibility.
Personal brand = the marketability and strength of your personal brand.
Visibility = visibility to your target market.
Social capital = the amount of social capital you have generated within your network.

Later on in the chapter we will show you how to calculate your opportunity score. Before we do this, we will look in detail at four ingredients for successful networking: credibility, personal brand, visibility and social capital.

Credibility

'It is about the afters. People don't give a damn about how fantastic you are, what reports you have, and if you phone people back in half an hour. They want to know at the end of the day whether you will deliver on what you say you are going to do.'

Gina Wadsworth, partner at Contact Consultants and BNI director

❝ Credibility is an intangible quality which is difficult to define accurately ❞

Credibility is an intangible quality which is difficult to define accurately as it means different things to different people. I personally define someone who is credible as a person who has developed a reputation as someone who 'walks the walk and talks the talk' *and* delivers on all their commitments. But Ivan Misner, founder of BNI, defines credibility as *'the quality of being reliable, worthy of confidence'*.[1]

Before someone is willing to risk their reputation by recommending you to someone within their network, they want to know that you are credible, i.e. committed, will conduct yourself appropriately and will be able to deliver on something they put you forward for.

Robin, a coach, had a friend called Steve who was a committee member of two local photographic clubs. Both clubs were small but had different kinds of members. One had a long, extensive history and an older membership; the other was much younger and had a good mix of ages. Steve was treasurer for one and secretary for the other 'because no one else would volunteer'. But holding committee posts in the two clubs was adversely affecting his credibility. You may be wondering why. His credibility was low because both clubs saw he had divided loyalties. Robin asked him, 'In your heart of hearts, what do you want to be doing?' Steve said, 'Taking good photos.' 'So, which club is going to provide you with the best stimulus for that?' 'The younger one.' 'So what are you going to do?' 'Resign from the other club!' Steve did that and his photos are now being critically acclaimed around the world. One photo has been viewed 21,000 times in its first few weeks on the internet.

Until you get the opportunity to actually win business or get an interview, like Steve at the photography clubs, your credibility is built up via the perception of your personal brand, and your behaviour and attitudes. For example, if you want to be seen as 'credible' when networking, you need to:

---

[1] 'Moving from visibility to credibility', http://businessnetworking.com

- do what you say you are going to do, e.g. phone people when you say you are going to
- arrive on time to meetings and events
- share client and customer success stories and testimonials
- have business cards with your contact details, plus details of your professional associations and memberships, professional qualifications and any awards won
- keep your messages consistent over time
- focus on building the relationship rather than selling
- find simple ways to help the person you are meeting, for example connecting them with someone in your network
- get introductions to people you want to meet from 'credible' people within your network.

Tip

When searching for a new job, have a set of business cards printed, clearly showing your contact details and URLs of your LinkedIn profile, blog and online CV.

I found my first coaching client, who was not an employee of my old employers, as a direct result of a recommendation from a partner within my old firm. This trusted recommendation helped my credibility and was a key factor in the client's decision to first talk with me and subsequently hire me as his coach.

Make sure that when you are out networking, you are focused on finding out 'who you know' rather than the heinous crime of selling. There is nothing quite as damning for your credibility than a sign on your forehead that says 'I am desperate for business' or 'I am selling'.

Your credibility is normally tested after a networking event or after meeting someone. Why? Remember that your credibility is directly linked to your ability to 'walk the walk and talk the talk' *and* deliver on all your commitments. Potential clients or employers are always looking for someone who is keen and eager to work with them. It may only be something small, such as sending a short email saying you enjoyed meeting them, but the small and often inconsequential stuff is taken as evidence of how you may behave if they hired or employed you. I was amazed, when I started face-to-face networking in earnest, how few people actually did follow up after a networking event. On the basis of my personal experiences, I can promise you that a simple email or handwritten note stating how much you enjoyed meeting someone will make you positively stand out from your peers.

For example, I suggested to one of my clients who was looking for a new job that she sent a short email to her interviewers after her interview, saying thank you for their time and how much she enjoyed meeting them. The interviewers delayed their hiring decision as they couldn't decide between her and another candidate. In the end my client got the job without the need for a further interview. Did the follow-up email tip the balance for my client? In all honesty we will never know, but I bet it helped!

Why a strong personal brand is essential for networkers today

'The fundamental purpose of brands is to create loyalty and preference over the long term.'[2]

Jez Frampton, global chief executive of Interbrand

When people buy professional services, they are generally buying a high-value product, service or person. For this reason there has to be a high degree of trust between the buyer and seller before the purchase will take place. This means that a potential buyer of professional services will prefer to act on a referral or recommendation from someone they know, like and trust before engaging in a conversation with a potential supplier. If you are fortunate enough to be recommended, it means they are placing trust in you, not the company that employs you. It's your personal brand that they prefer rather than your employer's brand.

The recent rapid growth and adoption of social media has led to people being able to quickly generate a strong online personal brand and rapidly communicate their brand's promise via word-of-mouth referrals. Social media is also enabling people to maintain networks vastly bigger than a network based on face-to-face interactions alone. Whereas only five years ago we may have had only one or two people within our network whom we would have been happy to recommend, today we are only one

❝ Investing time and energy in building your personal brand is essential ❞

---

[2] *Interbrand: Best global brands 2010 report*, www.interbrand.com/en/best-global-brands/Best-Global-Brands-2010.aspx

click or Google search away from generating five or six recommendations of people within our network. It's the strength and marketability of our personal brand which is the determining factor as to whether we will be the person that others recommend. This is why investing time and energy in building your personal brand is essential to networkers today.

What is a personal brand?

'A personal brand states exactly what you can do, refers to you by your own name and carries with it the domain within which you operate.'

Robert Watson, managing director, Managing Well[3]

A personal brand is made up of your personal vision and purpose, values, skills, knowledge, natural talents, beliefs and attitudes, i.e. your brand attributes and characteristics. However, when you think about hiring a person, you are not thinking about their vision or purpose but your perception of them, i.e. how they position themselves in your mind by the brand attributes they choose to display and communicate. For example, Sir Bob Geldof is *the* guy you go to when you have a *big* humanitarian cause needing *huge* efforts from people who aren't looking to profit from their contribution.

'Personal branding is the process where you figure out what makes you special and then communicate it to a specific audience.'

Dan Schawbel, author of Me 2.0: Build a powerful brand to achieve career success

There are four main ways that we position and package, i.e. communicate, our personal brand to people around us:

What you do

■ What service or product you provide.

■ The niche, sector or community within which you operate.

How you do it

■ What processes, systems, communication media you use.

■ Where you choose to spend time physically and virtually.

How you show yourself to the world

■ How you listen, e.g. are you truly listening or just waiting for a gap to get your point across?

---

[3] www.managingwell.com.au

■ How you choose to look and dress, e.g. dressing in a well-tailored suit forms an impression in someone's mind.

■ How you conduct yourself in a social setting, e.g. your social airs and graces.

■ The possessions you surround yourself with, e.g. your car, phone, laptop case.

■ Your body language.

■ How well you handle your emotions in professional situations, particularly when under stress, i.e. your emotional maturity.

How you let the world know about what you do

■ What you say, how you say it and how you sound saying it.

■ How and what you write.

■ How well you navigate the new standards in media, e.g. social networking, Twitter.

■ How much of your personal life and circumstances you choose to share.

Similar to a brand team deciding to reposition their brand, you can also reposition the perception of your personal brand. For example, when Margaret Thatcher was the UK leader of the opposition, she worked on her image, specifically her voice and screen image. Her advisors, who thought her voice sounded too shrill, suggested she undertake voice training to lower the pitch to make her sound more authoritative.

Tip

A great personal brand to cultivate as a networker is someone who is 'helpful', 'well connected' and 'delivers on their promises'.

Ideas and inspiration to help you strengthen your personal brand

Quick ways anyone can strengthen their personal brand

1 Circulate articles (linked to your personal brand) to your network.
2 Include links on your email and forum signatures to your online articles and blogs.
3 Look the part.
4 Do what you say you are going to do.

5 Be authentic and true to your values and passions.

6 Ask people close to you what are your strengths and particular talents.

Ideas to strengthen your brand within your own organisation

1 Opt for assignments and work which will showcase your strengths.

2 Volunteer for high-profile assignments.

3 Offer to deliver presentations both in-house and externally.

4 Ask for 360° feedback from influential partners and directors within your firm.

5 Spend time helping more junior members in the firm build their career.

6 Write articles for the in-house newsletter or blog.

7 Offer to become a mentor.

8 Get on an assignment which is being led by a known expert within your firm.

9 Routinely ask for feedback at the end of each assignment and share any positive feedback with people who have influence over your career.

Ideas to strengthen your personal brand outside your own organisation

1 Volunteer to be a guest speaker at networking groups and conferences.

2 Run training sessions and workshops on topics connected to your personal brand.

3 Find a mentor, outside your organisation, who is seen to be strong in the area which you want to become famous for.

4 Tweet about your area of specialism.

5 Have business cards printed with links to your online presence.

6 Record YouTube videos on subjects based around your personal brand.

7 Start a special interest group within your professional association.

8 Take a committee, moderator or board-level role within your professional association, special interest group or online forum.

9 Ask for testimonials and endorsements from experts within your field.

10 Register the domain name for your personal name and use it as your online CV.

How to use writing to strengthen your brand

1 Write articles for in-house publications, external magazines (print and online), newsletters or blogs.

2 Start a blog based around your personal brand.

3 Comment on blogs which are focused on your personal brand.

4 Submit articles to www.ezines.com and other online article sites.

5 Write an e-book or book.

6 Start writing a column for an internal or external print/online magazine.

7 Participate in online forums and answer questions based around your specialism.

8 Interview well-known experts in your field for your blog.

How to use LinkedIn to strengthen your brand

1 Start a LinkedIn group which enables you to showcase your expertise.

2 Answer LinkedIn questions which showcase your subject of interest.

3 Include presentations, videos, white papers and articles on your LinkedIn profile.

Visibility

'Visibility is the point when someone becomes aware of the nature of your business.'[4]

Ivan Misner, founder of BNI

> **Tip**
>
> When you join a formal networking group such as BNI or 4Networking, ask to do the member spotlight feature early into your membership.

First, what do we mean by being visible? Someone I used to work with called it 'top-of-the-mind' visibility, i.e. when someone within your network sees or hears of an opportunity, you are the first person they think of. With online networking giving people more choice over who within their network to recommend or contact, it has become easier to gain visibility with more people but harder to maintain 'top-of-the-mind' visibility with the people who are more likely to help you achieve your career or business goals.

To achieve 'top-of-the-mind' visibility, you could:

- regularly be present at local face-to-face networking events
- attend all the meetings of your formal networking club
- post on forums regularly
- update your status daily on social networking sites
- tweet regularly during the day
- send a regular newsletter to your network
- turn up to company formal and informal social events
- regularly send articles of interest to your network.

> **Tip**
>
> If you are new to an online forum, take the opportunity to introduce yourself to all the members of the forum. There is normally a section or pre-existing conversation where new members introduce themselves to the rest of the forum members.

---

[4] 'The first stage of the VCP process, visibility', http://businessnetworking.com

What is social capital?

'Ask not what your network can do for you, but what you can do for your network!'

Hamish Taylor, Shinergise Partners

Do you remember when you were at school and there was a boy or a girl who was incredibly popular? Everyone wanted to be their friend. These were the people who were always picked first for teams. Everyone seemed to know this boy or girl, and when they decided what they wanted to do, everyone seemed to want to do it with them. These people held great influence over the class. The most popular person at school had accumulated a large amount of what I am calling social capital.

> **Social capital can be measured by the breadth and the depth of your network**

Social capital is the imaginary bank account that you build up by being helpful to people. Social capital can be measured by the breadth and the depth of your network, the strength of your relationships within that network, and the goodwill and level of influence you have within that network.

The extent of your personal reach and your level of influence within your network, i.e. your social capital, will be key factors in whether you generate the opportunities you want and need from your network.

How to increase your social capital

Tip

To quickly increase your social capital, offer to take a position of responsibility within a committee, club or group which you belong to.

Similar to financial capital, social capital has to be earned and accumulated, but it can also be spent. The more deposits you make in your emotional bank balance with someone, the greater likelihood that your relationship will stay strong if you make a withdrawal later. It's the same with social capital – the more goodwill and influence you gain with your network, the greater the amount of social capital you are accumulating within your network.

Your level of social capital is enhanced by who you know and who you are seen with. If you spend time with people who have a greater level of prestige, credibility or status, some of that automatically rubs off on you. Let's say you wanted to join a charity but you weren't especially tied to any one cause. You look around, and the local cancer support group has three prominent business leaders on the committee. Spending time with these three prominent business leaders will help you increase your social capital.

To earn and accumulate social capital takes time and investment on your part. The most successful networkers use behaviours and attitudes which automatically build up their social capital with the right people in their networks. In the next section of this chapter we will look at the behaviours and attitudes which successful networkers consistently demonstrate.

Twenty quick and easy ways to increase your social capital with people in your network

1   Send a thank-you card or follow-up email after meeting them.
2   Call someone in your network.
3   Send a birthday, Christmas or 'well done' card.
4   Arrange a speaking engagement for them.
5   Make an introduction.
6   Pass on a referral.
7   Write a testimonial.
8   Write an article for them.
9   Post a blog written by them on your blog.
10   Put a link from your blog to their website or blog.
11   Connect with them on more than one social networking site.
12   Send an article of interest.
13   Nominate them for an award.
14   Vote for them in an award.
15   Send them a small gift.
16   Invite them to some corporate hospitality.
17   Include an article from them in your newsletter.
18   Help them with a query or question they have posted on a social networking site.
19   Have a one-to-one meeting with someone.
20   Bring along a guest to a networking meeting.

What one thing could you do today to increase your social capital within your network?

Measuring your opportunity score

As a general rule of thumb, the higher your opportunity score, the greater likelihood of success via networking. By measuring your opportunity score, you will be able to easily see where to place your effort to increase the number of opportunities you attract via your networking activities.

To measure your current opportunity score, look at Table 2.1 and score yourself between 1 and 5 for each of the four ingredients for successful networking: credibility, personal brand, visibility and social capital.

Table 2.1 Calculating your personal opportunity score

Score	Personal brand *The marketability and strength of your personal brand*	Visibility *Your profile among your target market*
1	You are not distinguishable among your peers	Your target market has never heard of you
2	You are known among your close network as 'the person' to talk to for 'y'	Your target market becomes aware of you
3	You have an active social media presence and are known among your wide network as 'the person' to talk to for 'y'	Your name is known within your target market and you may have a small following on social media (< 1000 followers)
4	You may have a book published and have a very active social media presence – via blogging and social networking sites. Journalists will occasionally quote you. Your personal brand is now becoming stronger than your business's brand	Your name is well known within your target market and you are likely to have a medium-sized following (2000 followers or connections) on social media
5	You have written books, published articles, appeared on TV, presented at major conferences and are a household name within your industry or area of specialism	Your name is widely known within your target market and you are likely to have a large following (10,000 followers or connections) on social media

Let's take a worked example. One of my business coaching clients, an HR consultant, wanted to significantly increase the number of referrals she generated via her networking activities. We calculated her opportunity score, using Table 2.1, and this was how she scored:

Social capital *The influence and reach you have within your network*	*Credibility* *The extent to which you deliver on your promises and 'walk your walk' and 'talk your talk'*
Influential only among relatives and immediate work colleagues	You have no track record in your specialist area and are unlikely to write or talk about your specialist subject
Strong influence of up to 50 people	You may write or talk about your specialist subject. Some people ask your opinion, but often they are asking others ahead of you
Strong influence of 51–150 people	You regularly write and talk about your specialist subject and are building up a small client list
Strong influence of 151 to 500 people	You write and talk about your specialist subject regularly and have a well-stocked client list, with a few people using you as a trusted advisor
Strong influence of more than 501 people	You are in constant demand to write and talk about your specialist subject. You have an impressive client list and there are many people who use you as a trusted advisor

Personal brand	2
Credibility	2
Visibility	2
Social capital	3
Opportunity score	14

After calculating her opportunity score, my client decided to focus her networking efforts to increase her credibility with her target audience. Six months later, her investment to increase her credibility with her target audience had paid off: her word-of-mouth referrals and recommendations had doubled.

> **❝You will gain ideas and inspiration to improve your own opportunity score❞**

As you read through this book, you will gain ideas and inspiration to improve your own opportunity score and become a more effective networker.

Summary

There are four ingredients needed for networking success:

■ credibility – the extent to which you deliver on your promises and 'walk your walk' and 'talk your talk'

■ personal branding – the marketability and strength of your personal brand

■ visibility – your profile among your target market

■ social capital – the influence and reach you have within your network.

Before someone is willing to risk their reputation by recommending you to someone within their network, they want to know that you are credible, i.e. committed, will conduct yourself appropriately and will be able to deliver on something they put you forward for.

A potential buyer of professional services will prefer to act on a referral or recommendation from someone they know, like and trust before engaging in a conversation with a potential supplier. As people's networks increase significantly in size due to the extra reach afforded to them by social networking, the strength of your personal brand will be a significant contributory factor in whether they contact you first.

Your personal brand attributes are your vision and purpose, values, skills, knowledge, natural talents, beliefs and attitudes. You position your personal brand in the minds of others by how, when and where you choose to communicate to others.

With online networking giving people more choice over who within their network to recommend or contact, it has become easier to gain visibility with more people but harder to maintain 'top-of-the-mind' visibility with the people who are more likely to help you achieve your career or business goals.

The extent of your personal reach and your level of influence within your network, i.e. your social capital, will be key factors in whether you generate the opportunities you want and need from your network.

By measuring and knowing your opportunity score, you know where best to expend your efforts to generate success via your networking activities.

ACTION POINTS

■ Identify the ten people who could have a positive impact on your business or career. Assess the amount of social capital you have with these ten people (low, medium or high). For anyone with whom you have low or medium social capital, identify ways to increase your social capital with them.

■ Ask three people close to you what you could do to increase the influence within your personal network.

■ Identify three ways in which you can increase and maintain your 'top-of-the-mind' visibility with people important to your career and business success.

■ Research where people who are important to your career or business success maintain an online presence.

■ Start writing articles for a magazine, blog or newsletter on topics based around your personal brand.

■ Identify three ways in which you may be damaging your credibility. Now commit to an action to change your behaviour.

■ After you have met someone, get into the habit of sending them a short email stating how much you enjoyed meeting them and asking them to connect with you on LinkedIn, Twitter and other social networks.

■ Ask your mentor or manager, or people you trust, for feedback on how visible and credible you are to senior managers, directors and partners within your firm.

■ Calculate your opportunity score and identify three simple ways in which you can increase your opportunity score.

Further resources

Books

Networking Like A Pro: Turning contacts into connections, Ivan R. Misner, David C. Alexander and Brian Hilliard, Entrepreneur Press, 2010.

Me 2.0: Build a powerful brand to achieve career success, revised edition, Dan Schawbel, Kaplan Trade, 2010.

E-book: How to build and define your own personal brand www.joinedupnetworking.com

Confident Networking for Career Success and Satisfaction, Gael Lindenfield and Stuart Lindenfield, Piatkus Books, 2005.

Brilliant Networking: What the best networkers, know, do and say, 2nd edition, Stephen D'Souza, Prentice Hall, 2010.

Blogs and websites

Joined Up Business Networking for Professionals http://joinedupnetworking. com

Dan Schawbel's personal branding blog www.personalbrandingblog.com

Ivan Misner's Networking Now blog http://businessnetworking.com

Andy Lopata's Connecting is not enough blog www.lopata.co.uk/blog

Rob Brown's blog www.rob-brown.com/Blog-Archive

3

Behave like a great networker

What topics are covered in this chapter?

- How to think and behave to gain success when networking
- The right attitudes needed to become a great networker

In the previous chapter you learned about the four essential ingredients needed to be successful at networking. But if you are going to build your credibility, visibility, social capital and personal brand you've got to behave and think appropriately. Networking with the right attitude is key – don't think of it as selling, although it may generate you sales ultimately. If you go in with a selling attitude, it will put people off wanting to develop a relationship with you. This chapter shows you how the right behaviours and attitudes will lead you to networking success.

Be selfless and generous

'The purpose of networking is to find out how you can help people and then help them.'

Jeremy Marchant, Emotional Intelligence at Work[1]

> The guiding principle of BNI, the world's largest business networking organisation, is Givers Gain®: the good you do comes back to you over the long term and often in indirect ways.

---

[1] www.emotionalintelligenceatwork.com

Good networkers believe in something called abundance, i.e. there is always enough to go around. Very often business people and job hunters believe the opposite is true, i.e. they assume that there is only a limited amount of business and jobs to go around. This can lead to competitive and aggressive behaviour, which damages credibility, reduces social capital and literally stifles opportunities from networking activities.

The abundance mindset generates opportunities due to the 'law of reciprocity'. Robert Cialdini, in his book *Influence: The Psychology of Persuasion*,[2] identified the 'law of reciprocity', i.e. that people are more likely to reciprocate if you do something positive for them first. Be aware that successful networkers, such as Jonathan Senior, managing director of Sharp End Training (www.sharp-end-training.co.uk), when he offered to host my new website for free, don't apply the law of reciprocity in a calculating way – it's not about expecting a quid pro quo. They know that if they help someone out, they will benefit at some point in a roundabout way – it just may not be directly from the person they helped out.

Be 'always open for networking'

> **Tip**
>
> Always have your business card with you. You never know when you may need it.

When I met Elinor Barbary in April 2010, her virtual assistant and personal concierge business, Barbary Solutions (http://barbarysolutions.com), focused on creative professionals, was three months old and growing rapidly. Elinor is a great example of someone who is 'always open for networking'. Even though I was interviewing her for research for my book, Elinor directly gained two new clients as a result of the introductions I gave her after our conversation. Great networkers, like Elinor, don't see any boundaries between their personal and professional lives, or online and face-to-face networking. They are literally always looking for opportunities to network and help someone. In the past six months, I've embraced this 'always open for networking' within my personal life. Like many parents with young children, I found attending birthday parties with my children a chore. I decided to view these parties as an opportu-

---

[2] Cialdini, R., *Influence: The Psychology of Persuasion*, revised edition, 1st Collins Business Essentials, 2007.

nity to meet some interesting people. As a direct result of this mindset change, I've recently met some new associates for The Efficiency Coach and potential clients when attending birthday parties and social events with my children.

Be interested in people first and foremost, business second

How many times have you been at an event and been pitched to? How did it feel? I bet you were thinking, how do I end this conversation and move on? Everyone hates being sold to. If you find yourself trying to convince someone to take up an opportunity, even a free opportunity, this is selling. Good networkers know that networking is not about selling, it's about getting to know people. Brad Burton deliberately built 4Networking with the principle that if you get to know people first, opportunities will follow. At 4Networking, unlike most formal networking clubs, you are not required to bring guests or referrals to every meeting but are given the opportunity to meet people and build relationships. The rapid growth of 4Networking within the UK demonstrates that this principle is working, as business is flowing between 4Networking members and their networks.

> **❝ Good networkers know that networking is not about selling ❞**

> **Tip**
>
> When meeting someone for the first time at a networking event, make sure you don't ask them first 'what do you do?' as this gives the impression that you are only interested in what you can sell to them. Instead ask them a question which shows an interest in them as a person, such as 'how's your week going?'

The questions that you use when meeting someone for the first time will often demonstrate to the person whether you are interested in them or their business. When you meet someone for the first time (unless they have specifically called a sales meeting), either online or in person, it is not the time or place to be using questions which qualify how ready they are to do business with you. This is selling, not networking.

Good questions which demonstrate your interest in them as a person could include:

- How long have you been in business?
- Tell me your story of how you came to be your own boss/in your current role/looking for a new role.
- How long have you been in your current role?
- What do you like about running your own business?
- What do you like about your current role or current employer?
- What prompted you to be your own boss?
- What prompted you to pursue a career as a …?
- What is your ideal or typical client?
- What are you looking to achieve at this event?
- If you could change one thing about your business/job, what would that be?
- When you are not working, what do you enjoy doing?

Be positive and enthusiastic

The best networkers attract people towards them, and they are the sort of people you enjoy spending time with. I found that the great networkers I spoke to in my research tended to be upbeat, positive and generally enthusiastic about the future and what it held for them. As a result it was easy to spend time getting to know them. Positivity and enthusiasm help to build up your social capital. The flipside is negative, apathetic and critical people tend to act like a drain on our emotions and energy, which leads to a reduction in their social capital. Who would you like to spend your time with, someone you feel good with or someone who drains the positive energy out of you?

Be focused and disciplined

> **Tip**
>
> Pick a maximum of three internet forums to maintain a presence in. Any more and you will spread yourself too thinly.

Great networkers, like Babs Morse, an image consultant (www.firstimpressionssandy.co.uk), love meeting and spending time with people. Babs learned the hard way that she needed to be focused when out networking. Too much networking without a purpose, while enjoyable, was costing her time and business. Babs now limits her networking to networking groups with a high percentage of her target market. She systematically tracks all her referrals and recommendations back to the source and networking group. Babs uses a simple spreadsheet to capture all her data on referrals; however, your customer relationship management (CRM) system may do this for you. She then uses this information to make decisions on whether to renew her annual membership to the six networking groups of which she is a member.

This takes discipline, and often a sizeable investment in time, processes and systems. Set yourself goals and targets similar to Bryony Thomas, chief clear thinker at Clear Thought Consulting Limited (www.clear-thought. co.uk). Bryony has a monthly handshake quota of ten people, i.e. within a month she will physically meet at least ten people who will benefit her or her business. How easy would it be for you to aim to meet one or two new people a month?

It's this focus and discipline which enables the best networkers to maintain an effective level of visibility at the forums, social networking sites and networking groups they frequent.

> **Tip**
>
> Eighty per cent of success from networking comes not from meeting new people but from maintaining contact with your existing network.

Cultivate a win–win mentality

When I started The Efficiency Coach, a coaching and consultancy company, I was given my first freelance opportunity by Alan Smith, of Alan Smith & Associates (www.alansmithassociates.com). I had first met Alan when he had run a team day for one of my internal client groups. Alan had asked to stay in touch (always the sign of a good networker!). As Alan's firm specialised in outplacement and career coaching, he was one of the first people I talked to when I realised I was going self-employed. I was interested to know what qualifications and experience I needed to work as a career coach in the outplacement sector. What started as a fact-finding conversation soon ended up as a hiring conversation, as Alan realised that I could help him out with one of his legal clients who wanted to do some leadership development work. When it dawned on me that Alan had a job in mind for me, I then introduced him to John Stylianou, one of my team members at the time, who was also leaving to go self-employed. This win–win mentality worked incredibly well in the short, medium and long term for Alan, John and myself. Both John and myself gained this and subsequent work from the conversation, and have worked together closely ever since. Alan ended up winning from the conversation as he gained a team of learning and development specialists, with credibility within professional services, to complement his firm's growing specialism in outplacement for professional services.

Networking works best when the people you are networking with have a collaboration mindset, i.e. they are always looking for the win–win. It's linked back to the abundance principle. If you truly believe that there is enough business (or jobs) to go around, you are always looking for a win–win outcome for the people within your network.

Be brave

'I don't have any qualms about dropping an email or a LinkedIn request to somebody who is quite high profile within my sort of industry. And as a result of that I have made very strong links with high-profile and influential people in my industry.'

Karen Spillane, training professional

> **Tip**
>
> If you want a highly influential member of your firm or business to be your mentor, just ask, and tell them why you have chosen them. Most people are flattered to be asked and will say 'yes'.

As we grow up we learn social etiquette but also form perceptions of people based on their position, perceived authority and experience. We can often fall into the trap of seeing the title rather than the person. Most conference speakers and industry experts are very willing to have a conversation with anyone who asks them. If you find yourself saying or thinking, 'I couldn't talk to them because ...', take a moment to think whether a young child would see any barrier to a conversation. If a young child wouldn't see a barrier, then you are applying an imaginary barrier, i.e. letting a self-limiting belief reduce the size and effectiveness of your

> ❝Great networkers see only the person, not the title❞

network. Everyone I interviewed for this book either self-selected themselves or readily made themselves available for an interview, regardless of their time zone, title or expert status. All I had to do was pluck up the courage to ask.

Great networkers see only the person, not the title, and are always brave enough to have the conversation which will make a difference to their career or business.

Be committed

Neil Ryder, my co-founder of The Executive Village, and I were looking through our LinkedIn contacts for a new accountant. As we were discussing suitable candidates, one of the main criteria for selection was commitment. How likely were they to follow through on their commitments?

When someone recommends you or gives you a referral, they are placing their reputation on the line for you. To risk their reputation or credibility for you, they want to know that you are committed for the foreseeable future to what you are doing, whether continuing within employment or your business's strategy and offering.

Be willing to experiment

The only things that are certain in life are change and uncertainty. Businesses grow or decline; people move jobs; networking groups change. New networking groups, events and social networking sites are springing up all the time. This means that new opportunities to network will always be just around the corner. It's this willingness to experiment which means that the great networkers always seem to know where to spend their time to get the best return on their efforts.

Be curious

'I have an insatiable curiosity about people and business.'

Melissa Kidd, networking coach and trainer[3]

The best networkers are inherently curious. They are curious about people, businesses and new experiences. This in-built curiosity helps them to seek

---

[3] www.melissakidd.co.uk

out opportunities, for example new networking groups or sites, for them-selves and others in their network, but also to find areas of common ground to build rapport with people they meet.

Be tenacious and persistent

Many people make the mistake of starting to invest in their network at the point at which they need it, such as at the start of a job hunt. I normally know when any of my ex-colleagues is thinking of leaving my old employer as they get back in touch with me! Good networkers are investing in their network all the time, rather than waiting until they need to call upon their network. Think of your network as a fruit tree. Similar to a network, a fruit tree starts from a seed and then branches out as it grows. A good fruit tree bears fruit year after year only if it is looked after and nurtured. A fruit tree often takes a minimum of three years before it will produce a large harvestable crop year on year. Before a tree has reached maturity, you will be disappointed if you wish to enjoy the 'fruits of your labour'. As with a fruit tree, your network needs time to grow and mature. It will bear fruits – referrals, opportunities and recommendations – only if you take the time to maintain and nurture it. This is why the best networkers are tenacious and persistent. Great networkers know that if they take the time to maintain and nurture their network, it will eventually consistently bear fruit.

Be authentic

As Dan Schawbel says in his book on personal branding, *Me 2.0*,[4] your rela-tionships, and therefore your social capital, depend on your authenticity. Great networkers achieve their results on the back of building up strong and 'real' relationships with the people they meet. This means that the more authentic you can be with the people you meet, the more likely it is that you will generate mutually beneficial relationships.

Seek first to understand

Gina Wadsworth, partner at Contact Consultants, an IT support business, is a director of three BNI groups and a member of a fourth. In the three groups she runs she does not openly talk about her business. However, because she always takes the time to listen, get to know and understand the members

[4] Schawbel, D., *Me 2.0: Build a powerful brand to achieve career success*, Kaplan Trade, 2010.

of her groups, she still gains referrals from all four groups, regardless of the role she plays in the group. This is no accident – consistent opportunities come through a network only when relationships have been built. After a while, the members Gina has spent the time with to truly understand their business reciprocate and are genuinely interested in Gina's business. This investment of time to listen and understand others is part of the reason why Gina's business, via a marketing strategy built solely on networking, has doubled its profits and turnover every year for the past four years.

In Chapter 9 we will look in detail at how you can quickly develop rapport and build strong relationships with the people you meet when networking.

Act like the host

When you are at a networking event, be it in person or virtual, you can choose to wait to be introduced or take the initiative and do the introducing. Social networks are now so big that it is normally ineffective to wait to be introduced. Great networkers seem to have no fear, and take the

❝Great networkers seem to have no fear❞

initiative and introduce themselves to the people they want to meet. For example, if you are at a social event, don't wait for your host to introduce you to people, introduce yourself to the other guests. For more advice on 'working the room', see Part 3 of this book.

Summary

The best networkers use these behaviours and attitudes to build their social capital, visibility and credibility:

- Be selfless and generous.
- Be always open for networking – no boundaries between personal and professional life, or online and face-to-face networking.
- Be interested in people first and foremost, business second.
- Be positive and enthusiastic.
- Be focused and disciplined.
- Cultivate a win–win mentality.
- Be brave.
- Be committed.

■ Be willing to experiment.

■ Be curious.

■ Be tenacious and persistent.

■ Be authentic.

■ Seek first to understand.

■ Act like the host.

ACTION POINTS

■ Look at the list of 14 ways in which great networkers think and behave. What are your top three strengths in this list? What are your three greatest weaknesses in this list? What can you do to improve on your weaknesses?

■ The next time you meet someone for the first time, take the time to listen to them and find out as much as you can about them. Notice how this conversation differs from your normal 'first' conversations.

■ Where can you use your personal network to help you achieve business or career success?

■ Look through your personal and professional network and find three people who would benefit from introductions to other people in your network.

■ Who would be your first-choice mentor? What's stopping you from asking them?

■ Look through your network, in particular the people who are most important to your business or career. How much do you really know about them as a person? Next time you see or talk to one of these people, take the time to find out more about them as a person.

■ Outside of your working life, identify where you have some opportunities to informally network.

■ Think about your personal circumstances and decide on a target number of new people and existing members of your network to contact or meet each month.

Further resources

Books

Get Off Your Arse, Brad Burton, 4Publishing, 2009.

Confident Networking for Career Success and Satisfaction, Gael Lindenfield and Stuart Lindenfield, Piatkus Books, 2005.

... And Death Came Third! The definitive guide to networking and speaking in public, Andy Lopata and Peter Roper, Book Shaker, 2006.

Brilliant Networking: What the best networkers, know, do and say, 2nd edition, Stephen D'Souza, Prentice Hall, 2010.

Influence: The psychology of persuasion, revised edition, Robert Cialdini, 1st Collins Business Essentials, 2007.

Blogs and websites

Joined Up Business Networking www.joinedupnetworking.com

Andy Lopata's Connecting is not enough blog www.lopata.co.uk/blog

Ivan Misner's blog http://businessnetworking.com

2

Online and face-to-face networking options explored

'In terms of business networking groups, I look at networks and I say they achieve one of four things. They are either there to increase your profile, build your community, help you equip yourself better or help you generate referrals.'

Andy Lopata, author of ... And Death Came Third!

There are myriad face-to-face and online networking options available to the professional today. However, when you are networking, you are doing one or more of the following things:

- increasing your profile
- helping you learn, find answers and tools to your problems
- generating referrals
- assisting you to build a community of like-minded people.

In the next three chapters we are going to look at all the different networking options available to you and how you can maximise your effectiveness in all four of the above at each different type of event.

In 'Further resources' at the end of the book there is a section with contact details of major face-to-face and online networking groups.

4

Face-to-face options

What topics are covered in this chapter?

- Where and when you should network in person
- How to maximise your effectiveness at a face-to-face networking event
- The pros and cons of each different type of face-to-face networking event

By the end of this chapter you will learn where you should network in person and how to maximise your effectiveness when networking in person.

You can literally network any time and anywhere. Very simply, you need only one other person to talk to be able to indulge in some face-to-face networking. Face-to-face networking is wider than just attending a formal networking event. For example, these are all places where you can network:

- formal networking groups and business clubs
- parent-friendly networking clubs
- professional association events
- drop-in events
- conferences
- training courses
- award evenings
- speed networking events
- job seekers' clubs
- mastermind groups
- community-related causes
- volunteering
- personal social events
- company social events
- chance meetings
- corporate entertainment
- private members' clubs.

Events and networking groups designed to generate referrals

These include:

■ formal networking groups and business clubs, e.g. BNI (www.bni.com) or 4Networking (www.4networking.biz)

■ 'women-only' formal networking clubs, e.g. Athena (http: theathenanetwork.com), Women In Business Network (www.wibn. co.uk)

What you can expect

In every town (and often village) in the UK there will be at least one business or networking club, which exists to help the members of the club form a referral network. Typically, a formal business networking group should yield a return on investment of at least 20 times the money you have paid to attend the group. It's no surprise, then, that networking and business clubs, catering to the needs of the small business owner, are everywhere you look.

These are small to medium-sized groups which meet regularly – some as much as once a week, others as infrequently as once a month. The meetings will generally last a couple of hours and mostly take place over breakfast or lunch.

The meetings are normally very structured and focused on referral generation. Typically, a meeting will comprise informal networking, a spotlight feature on one member's business and a round of elevator pitches. Normally each member will stand up and do a short pitch about their business and what help they are looking for from the group. These pitches are often known as a '60 second', 'monthly minute' or '40 second slot'. In Chapter 8, we talk about your pitch in more detail.

'It is not the person who you are sat in front of – they may not be able to afford your services. But they may know many people who can afford and want your services. That is the bit that most people miss when networking. Your aim is to connect with their network, not try to sell to them.'

Brad Burton, founder of 4Networking

Most of these groups charge an annual subscription as well as a small fee for each meeting. Expect to pay £500–£1000 per year for membership and meeting fees for one of these groups, although groups will normally allow you to attend as a visitor twice without having to formally join.

Many of these groups have a profession exclusivity policy – i.e. only one accountant, solicitor, business coach is allowed per group. Group members are expected to attend every meeting – or send a substitute in their place. Typically, the formal networking clubs and groups attract predominantly sole traders, micro-business owners and small businesses.

> **❝ Many of these groups have a profession exclusivity policy ❞**

What's the benefit of attending a referral generation group?

'Being active in BNI is like having up to 40 sales people working for you, because your fellow members will be carrying your cards and referring your business to people they meet, without you having to pay them any salaries or commission.'

www.bni-europe.com/uk/bni-experience.php

These groups allow members to pool their resources and share their networks, and become advocates and unpaid sales people for each other. Think how much more business you would gain with an ten extra sales people generating trusted referrals for your business.

'70% of all my new clients in my first six months of business came via my membership of Athena.'

Alicia Cowan, founder of Absolute PA[1]

As well as the primary benefit of generating word-of-mouth business, a referral generation group can often be a good source of support and encouragement.

What are the downsides of attending a referral generation group?

Success in a referral generation group relies on group members being well connected to your target market and being prepared to invest time generating opportunities for you. When you join a group, these two conditions are not guaranteed.

Many of these groups take place early in the morning – which excludes membership from parents with early morning childcare responsibilities. For example, I attended a 'Business 4 Breakfast' group which met at 06:45. (This sort of start time is very common for breakfast networking clubs.) Like many people, I was never at my best at this time in the morning, having woken at 05:45.

---

[1] www.absolutepa.com

To generate a steady stream of referrals from your referral generation group, attendance at every meeting is vital. When you add up both the membership and meeting fees, plus the cost of your time to attend the meetings and have regular one-to-one meetings with the members, a referral generation group is a sizeable investment in your business.

Many of these groups are very structured and governed by many rules, practices and policies. Some people think that these rules can often hinder collaboration rather than encouraging it. If the pressure of continually having to provide leads for a group is simply too much for you, then it is probably time to leave the group.

How to maximise your effectiveness at a referral generation group

Ideally, your referral generation group should be made up of members who are well connected to your target market. Choose a group which seems to be the best fit for your personal style, intended market and your time availability.

When you are attending as a guest, gauge how much business is being passed at each meeting. Before joining a group, arrange to meet the chair person of the group. Ask if they can show you the types of people who attend the meetings regularly. In my case, I am always interested in groups with accountants, lawyers and consultants.

> **Tip**
>
> Prepare your pitch in advance of the meeting. It's one less thing to remember to do before you set off for your group meeting.

Many people make the mistake of thinking that they will instantly generate referrals and leads when they join a referral generation group. You may be lucky, however; the members of the group need to know, like and trust you before they will consistently pass business your way – particularly if you sell a complex or high-value product or service. Take the time to meet each and every member personally to build a strong relationship with them. As relationships take time to form, it will be months rather than weeks before the group will consistently generate you referrals.

BNI calls it 'Givers Gain®' – this is the mindset that a successful networker will always be on the lookout for opportunities for others. If you have this mindset, then business almost always follows. The person within the group who works the hardest to find opportunities for the other members is probably also receiving the most opportunities passed their way.

It sounds slightly illogical, but the more specific you can be with your requests of the group, the more likely it is that members of the group will be able to help. For example, if you say 'I am looking for local businesses which would like to save money', you are unlikely to get a response, as every business owner needs to save money. If you say, 'I am looking for local businesses which are looking to move premises and want to save money on their legal bills', you are more likely to get productive responses. See Chapter 8 for more on effective pitching at a networking event.

'Great sales stories are short, with a beginning, an end and no middle.'
Richard White, author of The Accidental Salesman®: Networking Survival Guide[2]

Prepare short stories of how your firm or business has helped its clients or customers. When you are new into a referral generation group, you need to focus on building up your credibility with the group; these sales stories will help build that credibility within the group. Your sales stories may highlight why people choose you, why people carry on choosing your firm, what you do to make sure you go the extra mile for your clients and customers, how much time/effort/money you have saved for your client ...

Most groups have a business spotlight feature. This is where one member gets the opportunity to showcase their business in more detail to the whole group. As a new member into the group, the sooner you can get this business spotlight, the better. Any opportunity to educate and inform group members about your business will take you nearer to your first referral from the group.

❝The sooner you can get this business spotlight, the better❞

Generally, each referral generation group is 'run' by a few elected or unelected members. Officers often benefit from a reduced membership fee, as well as increased visibility from the membership of the group. The increased visibility, social capital and perceived level of trust, i.e. credibility that is placed on the officers of the group, tend to result in a higher level of referrals coming their way.

Tip

To get more people listening to your pitch, take the time to listen intently to their pitches.

[2] White, R. *The Accidental Salesman®: Networking Survival Guide*, Book Shaker, 2011.

When you join a referral generation group, first impressions are important. Consciously or subconsciously, the other members will be wondering whether you will fit in and whether you will be an asset to the group. One of the best ways to help create a positive first impression and generate trust from the existing members is to listen to them and take a very active interest in them and their business. To quickly gain the trust of your fellow members, you need to put your business requirements and needs on the backburner. A good networker, who has been talking about their business, will always then ask you how they can help you in your business.

To generate a referral from a member of the club, they need to have remembered you. This means you need to have achieved 'top-of-mind' visibility with them, i.e. when they hear about a problem or meet a client or contact, they think about you and how you could possibly help this person. For example, if you are a member of a business networking club which meets monthly, then if you miss one meeting, it will be two months before you get an opportunity to see the rest of the club. This is more than enough time for a member to forget about you and your business.

Business networking clubs can often attract members from all different walks of life. Indeed, many business networking clubs have an 'exclusive' profession policy and allow only one member from one profession. The members of the club will not know your business as intimately as you do. Therefore, you need to educate the members on what problems you and your firm solve, and how to be able to spot the signs that someone needs your services and when to step in to offer assistance – that offer of assistance, of course, being to call you. For example, if you are a private-client solicitor whose practice has a conveyancing speciality, you need the members of the club to know that your firm is great at helping people who are thinking of moving house.

Guests can be a valuable source of referrals and business for all the members of the group. Take your time to ask people in your network to join you at your business networking meeting. This will build up your social capital with both your guests and the other members of the networking club.

Tip

When a member sends a substitute to a meeting, take the opportunity to talk to them and get to know them. Substitutes tend to turn up only once to a group.

Events and networking opportunities designed to help increase your profile

These include:

- company social events, e.g. employee leaving party, ad hoc drinks after work
- speed networking events
- award evenings
- parent-friendly networking clubs
- drop-in events, e.g. Chambers of Commerce networking events.

What you can expect

This type of networking involves mixing and mingling. Unlike formal networking clubs there is normally only a light structure for the event. Sometimes these events may have a speech or presentation on a topic of interest to the participants at the event. Generally, although there are a few exceptions, these types of events don't tend to happen in the morning.

Parent-friendly networking clubs offer a way for parents who run their own business to network at a convenient time and place with other business owners. Typically, these organisations will offer a crèche facility, so that while you network, your child plays safely.

What are the benefits of attending profile-raising events?

While formal networking clubs tend to attract small business owners and sole traders, you could potentially meet anyone from any business at these types of events. Your local Chambers of Commerce networking events could be attended by senior decision makers from the local blue-chip companies as well as the sole traders. Or the managing director could pop along to your colleague's leaving drinks. These types of networking events are some of the few places you can meet senior decision makers or people who wouldn't normally go out networking.

What are the downsides to attending these types of events?

These events rely on you being prepared to go and talk to people at the event. There is a skill in being able to 'work a room' (see Chapter 10). Turning up

❝ Turning up to a networking event knowing no one takes bravery and courage ❞

to a networking event knowing no one takes bravery and courage. This irrational fear of having to talk to people you don't know is one of the most common reasons why professionals dread going networking.

With these types of events the attendance list is often very fluid. Sometimes you can verify the events attendance list in advance – but very often organisers won't know who is or isn't attending. This makes it very difficult to be able to focus accurately your networking time and efforts.

At these events you may bump into the professional who has been told by the firm to go out and network to drum up some business. Very often these professionals have not been trained to network and will go out and try to sell their services to everyone they meet at these events. If you have ever been sold to while out networking, you will know how painful it is.

How to maximise your effectiveness at these types of events

At these events you never know who you are going to meet and who will suggest that 'we get together for a longer, more in-depth conversation'. If you have had a good conversation with someone, inevitably they will ask you for your business card and permission to stay in touch. Saying you 'don't have a business card', 'have run out' or 'forgotten your business cards' is unprofessional and will damage your credibility. If you are in the midst of a career change or don't get provided with business cards by your organisation then get your own printed up.

> **Tip**
>
> Keep a small stash of business cards in your handbag, car, laptop bag and coat pocket. That way you will never be without a business card.

If you turn up early you have the opportunity to speak to people before the groups and closed conversations tend to form. I've noticed that the valuable conversations at networking events have a tendency to happen towards the end of the event. This is because there are fewer interruptions, everyone is more relaxed and people are less 'needy' to meet their quota of people.

'Before I attend any event, I will have identified and researched five people who I want to talk to at the event.'

Bryony Thomas, chief clear thinker at Clear Thought Consulting

Remember to prepare in advance of attending the event. For example:

> **Tip**
>
> Before you attend an event ask around your social networks to see who else is attending the event.

- Ask your host for a guest list in advance.
- Identify 3–6 people you want to have a conversation with.
- Do some research on the contacts you want to meet – what line of business are they in? What may be the particular business or personal challenges that they may be facing?

On the day before you go to the networking event, have a quick look at some of the online news websites and relevant trade journals, and formulate an opinion on some of the top stories.

Now, Mr Smith from Fantastic Widgets may not be your target client. But he may know someone who is. If you want to stay in touch, then ask for their business card. But it is more powerful to find a reason to stay in touch. For example, 'have you met so-and-so? – I'll send you their details', 'I was reading a great article – I will send you a copy'. This helps to build up your credibility and social capital with the person you have met.

In Chapter 3 we discussed how great networkers are focused and disciplined in their networking. Before you attend a profile-building event always give yourself a goal or objective for the evening. For example, this could mean, talk to one person within my target market and get permission for a follow-up meeting. This will help you make the most of any event you attend.

If there is someone on your list to meet at the event, ask your host to introduce you to them. It is very easy to get lost in a room full of people – and, if you are short like me, to be able to spot the people you have come to meet. A good host will normally be very happy to make the introductions for you.

Events and networking to help you learn, find answers and tools to your problems

These include:

- professional association events
- mastermind groups

- training courses
- conferences and seminars
- job seekers' clubs.

Professional association events

Professional associations will often host a series of events across the year which will be of interest and benefit to their members. Most of these events are free or heavily subsidised for their members. For example, if your business plan involved you meeting accountants, have a look at the events hosted by the Institute of Chartered Accountants in England and Wales (ICAEW). Members of professional associations may gain valuable continuing professional development (CPD) points as a result of attending their association's events. There is the opportunity to meet senior decision makers of mid- to large-sized companies at these events.

Mastermind groups

These are groups of business owners who meet regularly to provide input, ideas and suggestions to help each other achieve their business goals. Apart from The Executive Village, most formal mastermind groups normally charge a fairly high monthly membership fee, coupled with an expectation that all members of the group will attend all the meetings. Often mastermind groups are limited to one representative from each profession.

Training courses

These can be in-house or externally run training courses. Most training courses will include at least five people who are likely to be from a similar background to you. If you are on a residential course, it is a great way to make friends and strengthen relationships when you are bonding during your learning experiences.

Conferences and seminars

❝ Conferences and seminars are a great place to meet like-minded professionals ❞

Conferences and seminars are a great place to meet like-minded professionals – or find a large proportion of your target market in one place! They are a place where you can meet senior decision makers within micro, small, medium and large businesses. Normally conferences involve a programme of keynote speakers and smaller workshops, and exhibitors (who have paid to be at the event!).

Job seekers' clubs

These are formal or informal clubs set up to help job seekers support and actively help each other in their quest to find a new job. Of job seekers who use a job club to help them find a new job, 84 per cent find success via this route.[3]

What are the benefits of attending events which help you learn, and give you answers and tools to solve your problems?

The obvious benefit of attending these types of events is the opportunity to learn and gain valuable continuing professional development credits. Five years ago, I attended a two-day residential leadership course run by my previous employers, BDO LLP. At this course I met one of the BDO LLP's partners, Wendy. We stayed in touch after the course and Wendy's recommendation led to my first private coaching client. These events, while directly helping you learn, are good for helping you raise your profile within your current organisation. Training courses and mastermind groups, due to the time spent with participants, are great for helping you develop strong relationships quickly.

These types of events, especially high-profile industry conferences, often contain a high proportion of your target market – including many senior-level decision makers. For example, a seminar by a firm of accountants for potential and existing clients will always be very well attended by partners.

Mastermind events are a great way for you to demonstrate your credibility and gain valuable social capital by freely sharing your expertise. These events often give you an intimate view of someone else's business, which often leads to business being generated for participants.

What are the downsides to attending these types of events?

Often these events are time hungry. For example, most mastermind groups will demand a day of your time each month. A training course or conference could take you out of the office and away from client work for two

---

[3] Bolles, R. N., *What colour is your parachute?* Ten Speed Press, 2008.

or three days. Most of these types of events will provide only short blocks of time for informal networking as networking is not the prime purpose of the event.

How to maximise your effectiveness at an event to help you learn, find answers and tools to your problems

Speaking at conferences is a massive opportunity to build your personal brand and showcase your expertise. As a speaker at a conference, you are afforded a special status – making meeting influential people easier. Very often, your status as a speaker gives you instant credibility and social capital, meaning that attendees will go out of their way to talk to you and find out more about what you do. Often a speaker will get complimentary tickets to the conference. This is not always the case, as there are some trade shows which are now disguised as conferences, where the speakers, delegates and exhibitors pay for the privilege of being there.

Unlike a profile-building event, these events will always have a guest list which is almost always available before the event. If you have got the attendance list in advance it eliminates the need to hide in a corner to check the attendee list. If the first time you see the attendee list is actually on the morning of the event, then you are already at a disadvantage to the experienced networker. Most conferences I have attended are noisy and heaving with people, and it takes many calls and text messages to find someone you have already agreed to meet up with – let alone bump into one of your targets.

Always ask for the delegate list in advance of the conference – most hosts are normally happy to provide this on request – and use LinkedIn and Google searches to find contact details for the people you want to meet. Most people who are contacted in advance by other conference delegates are naturally flattered at the attention and pleased to have someone to talk to.

The way of increasing the odds of having a good conversation with someone you want to meet is to contact them in advance of the event and arrange to meet over lunch, a coffee break or a session that neither of you wants to attend in the formal proceedings. There is normally valuable networking time to be had before the formal part of the event starts and after the last formal session of the day. This is time when you could be arranging to meet people for a longer conversation. There is no reason why you have to stick slavishly to the formal agenda given to you at registration. Have you thought about organising your own dinner? Or hosting a discussion over lunch?

When you sit down for lunch, seminar, master class or presentation, you have a fabulous opportunity to strengthen the relationship with the person you are sitting next to. If you are on a training course, resist the temptation to always sit in the same place next to the same person. Push yourself out of your comfort zone and aim to sit next to a new person in each session. Try to avoid sitting with a colleague during a presentation or lunch – it is a waste of a good opportunity to bond with someone you've only just met. Five minutes before a formal session starts, ask your host to introduce you to one of the people you have come to the event to meet. You then simply say 'I've enjoyed our conversation, may I join you?' If you've made the right impression, the answer will normally be 'yes', and you now have a huge opportunity to build upon your initial conversation and develop a deeper relationship during the formal event proceedings.

Many people shy away from asking questions in sessions. Having been a guest speaker, I know that speakers want to be asked questions by the audience. There is nothing worse than finishing your presentation and no one asking a question! Asking insightful questions based around an area of your expertise is a great way to get noticed by the entire audience. It also gives you something to talk about when someone comes up to you later and says, 'That was an interesting question you asked'. When asking your question, make sure you remember to state your name, business and what you do clearly.

❝Remember to add people to your LinkedIn connections❞

Remember to send an email to all the people you have met at the event and follow up on your commitments to put some time in the diary to talk more. Remember to add people to your LinkedIn connections and start following them on Twitter.

Events and networking to help you build a personal community of like-minded people

These include:

- community-related causes, e.g. rotary club
- volunteering
- social events
- communal working groups, e.g. jelly groups
- corporate entertainment
- private members' clubs, e.g. 1, Alfred Place.

Community-related causes

These are groups of people who join together to support a community-related cause or shared mutual interest. These are normally good places to meet senior decision makers from mid- to large-sized companies who normally wouldn't be out networking. Examples of community-related cause groups are Rotary, a residents' association, choir, book club, football club, etc.

Volunteering

Giving up some of your time to help in a charity or school, or to run the local branch of your professional association, is still a form of networking. If you are looking to meet senior decision makers from mid- to large-sized companies then consider becoming a school governor or a trustee of a local charity.

Social events

These are events or get-togethers that happen within your social life. Friends' parties, children's play dates, family events are all places which you can network and find opportunities.

Communal working groups

These are groups of people who meet up to work together, for example jelly groups (www.workatjelly.com). While their primary purpose is to provide company for people who normally work alone, they are a great way to meet other professionals and sole traders.

Corporate entertainment

This is where a supplier or client, or someone in the business world who wants to get to know you better, 'treats' you to a meal out, or a ticket to a cultural or sporting event. You could find yourself enjoying a seat in a box at the opera, or a corporate entertainment box at a football or rugby event.

Private members' clubs

These are places where like-minded people meet. Membership of these clubs is normally on a strict invitation-only basis, with rigorous vetting procedures for potential members. Your club membership is often based on your level of seniority, family status or personal connections.

What are the benefits of attending community-building events or groups?

These types of events, opportunities and places are a great way to network when you have no time to network, especially if you are using your network to help you find your next role.

What are the downsides to attending these types of events?

The primary purpose of this type of event is not networking. Each type of community-building event or occasion will have an implied social etiquette which you will need to conform to. Focusing too much on a person's business interests at a family event will make the other guests feel awkward and reduce your social capital.

How to maximise your effectiveness at an event to help you learn, find answers and tools to your problems

I'm sure we have all experienced formal social occasions where we know only a handful of people. At a typical wedding you will know fewer than half the guests and the other half are an unknown quantity. Remember to circulate at these events, and as well as potentially meeting some great new people, you will lessen the risk of getting stuck talking to your Great Auntie Mary. Setting yourself a goal or objective for these events will help to push you out of your comfort zone and circulate.

❝Remember to circulate at these events❞

If you have met someone at a social event who you would like to help you achieve your business or career goals, don't talk too much business at the event, book a follow-up conversation or meeting.

There are often strict, unstated cultural rules or etiquette at a social event or club. For example, a female walking through the men-only lounge of a very traditional golf club could result in her club membership being withdrawn. Find out from your host what rules or traditions you will be expected to observe at the event or occasion. Be aware that your host may have other things happening later in the day – or may want to get to bed early. Listen out for clues when it is time to leave – for example, your host yawning. Overstaying your welcome is a great way to reduce your social capital!

Summary

There are many different ways you can network in person:

- formal networking groups and business clubs
- parent-friendly networking clubs
- professional association events
- drop-in events
- conferences
- training courses
- award evenings
- speed networking events
- job seekers' clubs

- mastermind groups
- community-related causes
- volunteering
- personal social events
- company social events
- chance meetings
- corporate entertainment
- private members' clubs.

To choose the right time and place to network in person, you need to answer the following questions:

- What's my primary purpose for going networking?
- How will this event, occasion or group help me achieve my career or business goals?
- How much time and energy can I invest in the club, group or occasion?

To maximise your effectiveness at the networking event, group or occasion:

- Always have your business cards with you.
- Make time for a follow-up conversation or email.
- Find a reason to stay in touch.
- Observe the social etiquette of the occasion or club and don't overstay your welcome.
- Give yourself goals for the event.
- Don't sell at an event – use an event to start and strengthen relationships.

ACTION POINTS

■ Submit the following terms into Google *xxxx + business networking*, where xxxx is the name of your local town, to find a list of networking groups which meet locally to you.

■ Access your professional association's website and see what events it is hosting which you would enjoy and benefit from attending.

■ Create your own or join a mastermind group, such as The Executive Village.

■ Commit to attend one face-to-face networking event in the next month. Before you attend the event, decide on your personal goal for the event.

■ Find out where the 'rain-makers' in your firm and your competitors' firms spend their time networking in person.

■ Identify an organisation, outside of work, which you would enjoy spending time in to increase your personal network. For example, an arts, music or sports club, Rotary, Round Table, Lions, school governorship, charity, etc.

■ Update your status on Facebook, Twitter or LinkedIn before you next go networking to see who else is attending.

■ Next time you go to a networking event, request the attendance list in advance and make contact with three people at the event before you go.

Further resources

Books

Never Eat Alone: And other secrets to success, one relationship at a time, 2nd edition, by Keith Ferrazzi, Doubleday, 2011.

Networking Like A Pro: Turning contacts into connections, Ivan R. Misner, David C. Alexander and Brian Hilliard, Entrepreneur Press, 2010.

Websites and blogs

The Executive Village www.executivevillage.co.uk

Joined Up Business Networking www.joinedupnetworking.com

Referral generation groups

BNI www.bni.com

4Networking www.4networking.biz

Athena http://theathenanetwork.com

Women in Business Network www.wibn.co.uk

Organisations which run regular networking events

Local Chambers of Commerce

Institute of Directors www.iod.com

Professional associations

Federation of Small Businesses www.fsb.org.uk

Parent-friendly networking groups

Mums the boss www.mumstheboss.co.uk

Mums Business Clubs http://mumsbusinessclub.com

Communal working groups

Jelly groups www.workatjelly.com

5

Online networking options

What topics are covered in this chapter?

■ The types of informal and formal online networking

■ What we mean by a social networking site and a micro-blogging site

■ How to generate referrals using online networking

■ How to maximise your effectiveness while networking online

In the previous chapter we looked at all the different face-to-face networking options available to today's professionals. All of these options require the networker to be physically present with another person. What happens when you have the motivation to network, but not the opportunity or time to go out and meet people? Or what happens if your target market does not reside locally to you? This is where online networking has the advantage over face-to-face networking.

Online networking lets you network all day and night, regardless of where you are in the world and who you are with. All you need is an internet connection or 3G signal – you don't even need someone else online at the time to network.

There are many different forms of online networking:

■ Twitter

■ social networking sites, e.g. LinkedIn, Facebook, Ecademy, Ning private networks

■ online forums.

Similar to face-to-face networking, these different types of online networking help you do one or more of the following things:

■ improve your profile, i.e. being 'found'

■ generate opportunities such as a new job or new clients

■ extend and strengthen the community around you

■ find solutions.

There are literally millions of social networking sites and online forums on the internet. Each site and forum will have its own focus, community, culture and social etiquette. In this chapter I will be talking about the most widely available ones which will have the most impact on your networking activities.

The world of social media is changing rapidly. In just the time it takes to write this book and publish it, there is a strong likelihood that there could be a new social networking site which has grown to become a major player. Don't believe me? Well, in April 2009, Twitter had 10 million accounts and this jumped to 70 million accounts within three months. In the process, it cemented its place as a major force in social media. Three years ago it would have been unthinkable to write about social networking without heavily featuring the biggest social networking site MySpace. Fast forward to now and Facebook has overtaken MySpace in popularity and is continually evolving – and from its roots in school and university networks is now a legitimate tool for business networkers.

In this chapter we will look at what I call my big three of online networking sites – LinkedIn, Twitter and Facebook. In fact, the combination of these, with a blog, is what will deliver a huge impact to you and your business, and should be your focus when you start online networking. In the next chapter we will look at how to use a blog as a business networking tool.

Generating referrals using online networking

Unlike BNI groups, there is no such direct equivalent of a referral marketing organisation in the online networking world. By this I mean no large formal or commercial platforms or communities where groups of like-minded individuals from different professions get together to generate referrals for each other. However, the opportunity score equation, as I have proved within my own businesses (see page 16), still works for online networking – i.e. the more time you invest in demonstrating your credibility, helping others, building a consistent and marketable personal brand and being visible to your target market, the more likelihood there is that opportunities will come your way via your online network.

Make it consistent

Consistency, just like integrity and reliability, is very important in the virtual world, as it forms the basis of trust in an online relationship. Trust takes longer to build up and is quicker to destroy within the virtual

❝Trust takes longer to build up and is quicker to destroy❞

world. Make sure the messages on your website, Twitter biography, Facebook page, LinkedIn and other online sites where you maintain a profile are all consistent. For example, you should use the same avatar for each online profile.

What is a 'social networking' site?

'Social media is collections of data and information, whereas social networking is collections of people.'

Peter Rees, E-marketing Systems[1]

A social networking site is a type of 'social media' – however, the terms social media and social networking are wrongly used interchangeably. A social networking site exists to connect people together to form an online community.

A social networking site tends to include the following pieces of functionality:

- user profiles
- a way to connect between users, e.g. Facebook 'friends', LinkedIn 'connections', Twitter 'followers'
- forums where users can post up and join in discussions
- a place for users to blog
- articles – normally written by the users
- groups or communities of users – for example, the LinkedIn groups
- private or open messaging between users
- SMS online chat between site users
- a status update or facility to share your thoughts with all the site's users.

[1] http://emarketingmatters.co.uk

For example, UK Business Forums (www.ukbusinessforums.co.uk) is one of the UK's biggest forums for entrepreneurs and business owners. Although it is a social networking site, it is best known for its busy and vibrant forums.

For a list of major social networking sites and online forums, please see, 'Further resources' at the end of the book.

LinkedIn

What is LinkedIn?

Tip

If you use only one social networking site or social media tool, then choose LinkedIn.

LinkedIn is a social networking site and has been described as 'Facebook for professionals'. At the time of writing, 75 million professionals in more than 200 countries are on LinkedIn. This figure is growing rapidly. If Twitter is the online networking equivalent of being in the world's largest bar, and Facebook is where you relax after a hard day at work, LinkedIn is where you go when you are at work. In other words, LinkedIn's culture is very professional, and to use LinkedIn effectively, your updates, questions and presence need to be professionally rather than personally orientated.

LinkedIn can be used as a contact book, CV, references book and a place where you can learn from your peers and connect with potential clients.

What are the benefits of using LinkedIn?

LinkedIn enables you to establish a professional profile on the web. If you Google your name, your LinkedIn profile will normally be returned in the first page, and unless you have a heavy online presence, within the top three results in Google. This means that your LinkedIn profile is likely to be the first place where someone checks out your online identity, i.e. the all-important 'first impression'. LinkedIn enables you to control this 'first impression'.

LinkedIn is one of the places where headhunters and recruiters looking for professionals search for candidates. They will either use LinkedIn to supplement their own candidate database, or LinkedIn has become their candidate database. Only yesterday I was contacted by a recruiter who had

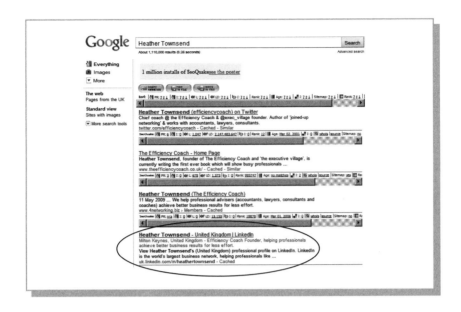

searched for 'leadership' + 'learning and development' on LinkedIn, and I had turned up in his search.

'We have gone from job searching to people searching.'

Dan Schawbel, author of Me 2.0

In today's fast-changing world people move jobs and locations constantly. After you have left an organisation it can be difficult to maintain contact with the network from your old organisation. Once you are on LinkedIn and connected with others, you remain connected to them even when they change their job and move to the other side of the world.

LinkedIn is a great way to find experts and solutions to your problems, using two specialist forum tools. The LinkedIn Answers allows you to pose questions to the LinkedIn community – which are normally answered promptly. To strengthen my brand as a business networking expert, I aim to answer nearly every genuine question within the professional networking Answers section. I noticed that Hamish Taylor,[2] MD at Shinergise, was also answering the same questions as I was, and was very knowledgeable about business networking. I requested to connect with him and interview him for the research for my book. As a result of this

> **LinkedIn is a great way to find experts and solutions to your problems**

---

[2] http://uk.LinkedIn.com/in/hamishtaylor

connection and subsequent conversations, Hamish has been an invaluable source to me on networking across different international cultures.

LinkedIn allows you to start up groups, as well as join groups. Each group membership is based around a particular theme or purpose. The communities within these groups are great places to ask questions, demonstrate your credibility and find help.

Companies and organisations are now able to have a presence on LinkedIn. Similar to Twitter, LinkedIn members can now 'follow' a company. This allows them to see company news or when someone has been promoted, been hired or left. If you are interested in working for or with an organisation, this functionality enables you to target the organisation effectively – or even anticipate a vacancy which will be of interest to you. Many companies, such as the publisher of this book, Financial Times Prentice Hall, are starting their own communities on LinkedIn by setting up a LinkedIn group for suppliers, clients, authors and advocates.[3]

LinkedIn allows you to search its database for users and organisations. You can see how you are connected to people who can have a positive influence on your career and business – and then get introductions via your network to these people. Great if you are looking for a new job or new business opportunities.

How to maximise your effectiveness on LinkedIn

Like any social networking medium you need to first decide why and how you will use LinkedIn to advance your career or business. For example, if you decide you want to change your current role you need to have decided on what role you are looking for. It is no good branding your LinkedIn profile for a role within a professional practice if you decide you want to go in-house. Bryony Thomas, chief clear thinker at Clear Thought Consulting, uses LinkedIn to maintain relationships with people clients and suppliers she has worked with and would recommend to others.

Your LinkedIn profile is your shop window to the world. You need to make sure your profile is displaying the 'goods', i.e. your brand, which you want potential clients or recruiters to buy from you. You are more likely to be found and contacted on LinkedIn if you fully fill out your profile. People still want to buy people – and if they get a truer sense of who you are via

---

[3] www.linkedin.com/groups?home=&gid=1910576&trk=anet_ug_hm&goback=.gdr_
1287312887164_1

your LinkedIn profile, they are more likely to choose to make a connection with you.

The more content on your profile which enhances your credibility – e.g. recommendations, 'best answers' on LinkedIn Answers, presentations and documents on your specialist subjects – the more opportunities that are likely to come your way.

LinkedIn can be your very own micro-PR machine. Regularly tell potential employers, clients and recruiters what you have achieved or are doing in the course of your normal working life. For example, via the status update function, tell people about great client wins, new recommendations, product or service launches, networking meetings you are attending.

To attract opportunities via LinkedIn you need to be a real person, not just a name in someone's contact list. As relationships, trust and credibility develop quicker in the real rather than the virtual world, always aim to take the important relationships out of LinkedIn and into the real world.

Twitter

What is Twitter?

If Facebook and LinkedIn are the adults of the social media revolution, Twitter is still very much the teenager of the family. But like most teenagers it has ripped up the rule book and become a major tool for any serious business networker.

Many people have dismissed Twitter as just boring, trivial chat. Who wants to know what you ate for lunch? It is true that much of the conversation on Twitter is fairly mundane. However, if you were at a mix-and-mingle net-working event, I'm guessing that most of your conversation that evening would be fairly mundane and classed as trivial chit-chat.

Twitter is a micro-blogging site. Users of the service (often called 'peeps' or 'tweeters') post short messages, called 'tweets', of up to 140 characters in length. Users choose to follow people or lists of people. Following means that you see all of their updates or 'tweets'.

Within Twitter you can privately message another person or 'peep' as long as they follow you, and you can send an open message or reply to any other 'peeps' as long as you know their Twitter name. Unless you choose to protect your tweets, so that only people you have approved can see them, everyone can see everyone else's tweets.

What are the benefits of using Twitter?

Twitter gives you an instant international reach and visibility. Unless you have protected your tweets, i.e. they will not show up in the public time-line, your tweets can be seen by anyone, anywhere, at any time. At the time of writing I have more than 5500 followers, who are spread all over the world, but mostly within the UK. Every time I tweet there is a possibility that 5500 people who follow me will see that tweet. Be warned, though, that if you say something stupid or insulting on Twitter, a lot of people may see it and spread it, before you can erase it.

❝Twitter gives you an instant international reach and visibility❞

The visibility and accessibility of Twitter means it is a great tool to drive traffic to your website. When I started the Joined Up Business Networking (www.joinedupnetworking.com) blog, I needed to generate traffic quickly to the blog – and did not want to wait for the search engine optimisation to kick in, or to pay for web traffic. By writing and publishing a blog post every day, and tweeting once about the new blog post, I generated 1000 visitors to the website in the first month it was up.

Twitter is sometimes referred to as an open networking tool: everyone can contact everyone else, regardless of status or prior relationships. If you are enjoying reading this book, how about sending me a tweet?[4] It's this acces-sibility which enables you to quickly and effectively find and connect with your target market. For example, when I started on Twitter I deliberately began to follow accountants and lawyers. This was how I found and 'met' Chris Sherliker,[5] managing partner of Silverman Sherliker LLP. Six months later, Chris became one of my first clients sourced from Twitter.

How to maximise your effectiveness on Twitter

Unlike LinkedIn, where the site's etiquette expects professional rather than personal updates, to use Twitter effectively you need to be the 'whole' person. So, what do I mean by the whole person? If you were networking at a large mix-and-mingle type of event, you would be rapidly bored by anyone who only talked work and didn't disclose their personal side or bothered to listen to what you had to say. It's the same with Twitter. People want to get to know you as a real person, and you will be more effective on Twitter if you talk about both the personal and professional parts of your

---

[4] www.Twitter.com/HeatherTowns and www.Twitter.com/joinedupnetwork
[5] www.Twitter.com/london_law_firm

life, and engage with people. This means that you need to fill out your bio and include a good, professional-looking picture within your profile.

> **Tip**
>
> Within your bio include keywords containing your target market, e.g. 'I work with accountants and lawyers'.

'To succeed on Twitter you need to show your whole personality and engage as an individual.'

Brian Inkster,[6] Inksters Solicitors

Twitter can very easily be used ineffectively as a networking tool. Before you start tweeting, it is essential that you know what you are trying to achieve by being on Twitter. For example, if you want to build relationships with people within your target market, you need to be actively looking to follow and engage with your target market on Twitter.

> **Tip**
>
> To use Twitter to build up your personal brand and credibility, regularly tweet out links to articles on your blog.

It's very easy to get seduced into trying to build up a follower base fast. It's not the number of followers you have that counts; it's the number of engaged followers you have.

To find out how engaged someone's follower base is, take a look at the number of lists which they have been included on. The higher the number of lists someone is included on, the greater the level of engagement within their follower base.

Facebook

What is Facebook?

Facebook is currently the biggest social networking site, with, at the time of writing, more than 500 million active users. This is equivalent to one in every 14 people in the world using Facebook. Facebook users can add

---

[6] www.Twitter.com/brianinkster

people as friends and send them messages, and update their personal profiles to notify friends about themselves. Facebook is a site rich with functionality, and users, through their Facebook profile, can post videos, links, updates – even play online games with their friends.

Although Facebook is a purely 'social' network – this is where people let their hair down at the end of the day – it does have a place in the professional's business networking toolkit. For example, if you are using your personal and professional network to job hunt, Facebook is a place where you can quickly contact your personal network. Look through any user's 'friends' and you will normally see a high proportion of people they are currently working with, or have worked with in the past.

❝Facebook is a place where you can quickly contact your personal network❞

Many firms and businesses see Facebook as a distraction from work and will routinely block employees' access to Facebook on company systems. However, in the past two years Facebook has evolved into a true business tool, so I expect that we will see more businesses opening up access to Facebook to their employees. Plus, mobile phone technology is now such that most people can access Facebook via their smartphone rather than relying on their company's IT systems.

What are the benefits of using Facebook?

Facebook is huge. Any adult between the age of 18 and 55 who is not on Facebook is now in the minority. Connecting with someone on Facebook is rapidly becoming the preferred mechanism for staying in touch with someone you like.

Facebook allows you to have business pages as well as a personal account. I have set up business pages for both 'Heather Townsend – writer, speaker and coach'[7] and 'The Efficiency Coach'.[8] These two pages have allowed me to build up a community of interested and engaged people on Facebook.

One of the hidden benefits of Facebook is its ability to help you strengthen your search engine optimisation for your website. As Facebook is ranked very highly by Google, any links from Facebook to your web page will boost the ranking for that page.

---

[7] www.facebook.com/TheHeatherTownsend
[8] www.facebook.com/TheEfficiencyCoach

How to maximise your effectiveness on Facebook

To get the most out of Facebook, you need to decide how you want to use it. It's absolutely fine to just use Facebook for purely social reasons – and that's all many professionals use it for.

Facebook is a different communication medium to LinkedIn or Twitter. What works on LinkedIn and Twitter won't always work on Facebook. For example, on Facebook people tend to update their status once or maybe twice a day. If you are a regular tweeter and tweet ten or more times a day and decide to display your tweets via Facebook (or LinkedIn, for that matter), it's a quick way to annoy your connections.

Tip

If you want to use Facebook as a business development tool, then use a business page to do this. Your personal network on Facebook will rapidly become fed up with reading your marketing updates on their Facebook stream.

To promote engagement with the people who 'like' your business page, remember to update the status once or twice a day, and keep the updates very chatty and personable. People want to be entertained on Facebook rather than 'sold' to.

Online forums

What are online forums?

These are websites where registered users can post up discussions or con-tribute to discussions by replying to the original post. Most online forums are part of a bigger social networking site. For example, a Facebook business page or private Ning network comes with its own online forum integrated. In fact, many social networking sites, e.g. UK Business Forums (www.ukbusinessforums.co.uk) are better known as an online forum rather than a social networking site.

What are the benefits of using online forums?

Online forums are a great way to connect and demonstrate your cred-ibility with your target audience. Most industry sectors and special interest groups have a forum somewhere dedicated to them and their particular requirements.

Online forums are a great way to find answers. I regularly use LinkedIn Answers, a specialist forum within LinkedIn, to help me with research.

How to maximise your effectiveness with online forums

You will achieve work and referrals via business forums only if you are prepared to be helpful and share your specialist knowledge. When answering a question on a forum, remember to read the question properly and answer the question (and subsequent questions asked in the threads). Building up a consistent track record for sharing your knowledge helps you build trust and credibility with the forum's users.

Trust and credibility are vital for you to gain work via the connections you have made on an online business forum. Everyone is aware that an online connection may not be who they say they are. This is often the reason that it takes longer to develop relationships, and ultimately business, via your online rather than offline networking. You gain credibility and trust if you are connected to your online contacts on more than one online forum or platform.

❝You are aiming to interact with people and build up a relationship❞

Remember that when you are on an internet forum, you are aiming to interact with people and build up a relationship. By freely offering your contact details, you will be surprised how many people do contact you directly. A relationship normally develops quicker if you take it offline, e.g. a phone call or face-to-face meeting.

Business-orientated internet forums are not the place to sell. I'm serious. Don't sell. When you are out networking, how much do you hate being sold to? It's the same on forums. Forum users can spot this a mile off. Posts like this (with no helpful information) …

'I've got loads of experience with your problem, give me a call on xxxx xxxxx, and I will talk you through it'

… are selling, and tend to infuriate people rather than showcase your expertise and credibility.

Many forums will let you put a standard email signature onto the bottom of all your posts, plus include links in your general text. This is fantastic for search engine optimisation. What keywords are important to you? How can you incorporate these keywords into a phrase which will entice people to click onto the link through to your website? For example, instead of hyperlinking 'JS Accounting Services' back to your website, what about 'find out how to save up to 20 per cent off your accountancy bills'.

Different groups of people frequent different forums. To maximise your effectiveness on forums you need to make sure you are in a forum with people you would like to meet. For example, if you want to meet female entrepreneurs, work-at-home mums or start-up businesses (run by females) then you want to hang around in the Everywoman site (www.everywoman. com). If you want to meet business owners with a significant overseas membership then UK Business Forums is a good place to hang out.

Each forum attracts different types of people and each site will have its own way of doing things. I maintain a heavy presence on three different business forums and they are like chalk and cheese. Two of these sites are heavily moderated and any selling or misuse of the forum is quickly curtailed. The other site is more tolerant of some light advertising by members.

To help you achieve an effective level of visibility on a forum, turn on the daily digest facility. This facility enables you to monitor conversations rather than having to go into the forums and 'hunt' for new conversations.

Summary

There are millions of online networking sites, but serious business networkers need to maintain a presence on LinkedIn, Twitter and Facebook. These three sites will generate profile, i.e. visibility, for you.

The etiquette of each social networking site is different. Savvy networkers take the time to understand the subtleties of each site and how to use it effectively.

You only need an internet connection to network online. As trust takes longer to build using purely online networking, aim to take the relationship offline to generate a stronger, deeper relationship more quickly.

When networking online, make sure you take the time to 'engage' with the people you are connecting and tweeting with.

ACTION POINTS

■ Join LinkedIn, Twitter and Facebook.

■ Write a short and a long bio about you for your online profiles. A short bio is normally limited to fewer than 200 characters.

▓ Find a decent professional head-and-shoulders shot of yourself to use on your online profiles.

▓ Find out on which sites your target market hangs out online. Register for these sites and set yourself a goal of visiting them daily and posting something on the site every day.

▓ Fully complete your LinkedIn profile and brand it for the job you want rather than the job you have now.

Further resources

Books

This Is Social Media: Blog, tweet, link your way to business success, Guy Clapperton, Capstone, 2009.

Me 2.0: Build a powerful brand to achieve career success, revised edition, Dan Schawbel, Kaplan Trade, 2010.

Socialnomics: How social media transforms the way we live and do business, 2nd edition, Erik Qualman, John Wiley & Sons, 2010.

Social Media 101: Tactics and tips to develop your business online, Chris Brogan, John Wiley & Sons, 2010.

Inbound Marketing: Get found using Google, social media and blogs, Brian Halligan and Dharmesh Shah, John Wiley & Sons, 2009.

Get up to Speed with Online Marketing: How to use websites, blogs, social networking and much more, Jon Reed, Financial Times Prentice Hall, 2010.

Websites and blogs

LinkedIn and Twitter training www.joinedupnetworking.com

The Efficiency Coach on Business Efficiency http://business-efficiency. theefficiencycoach.co.uk

Just Professionals www.justprofessionals.net

Chris Brogan's blog www.chrisbrogan.com

Mashable http://mashable.com

Social networking sites

For a list of major social networking sites see 'Further resources' at the end of the book.

6

Blogging

What topics are covered in this chapter?

- What is blogging?
- How to use blogging to enhance your credibility and personal brand

In the last chapter, we discussed the three main online networking sites, LinkedIn, Twitter and Facebook. These sites give you profile and visibility, but the impact of these sites is significantly heightened when used in conjunction with a well-written blog. It's the blog which gives you credibility and communicates your online personal brand to your audience. When you combine an active presence in online networking sites with a well-written blog, you are generating all four of the ingredients, as discussed in Chapter 2, needed for networking success: credibility, personal brand, visibility and social capital. In this chapter we show you how to use a blog as a networking tool and how to use it effectively in conjunction with your online networking activity.

Blogging

What is blogging?

A blog is a form of website where you can self-publish articles without needing the approval of anyone else. The prospect of being able to publish anything and everything may be very appealing to you; however, as a networker, your aim is to write intelligent and thought-provoking pieces which establish your

❝Your aim is to write intelligent and thought-provoking pieces❞

credibility as an expert in your specialist subject, and invite people to interact with you on your blog.

A blog post is not like a magazine article or feature. The ideal length of a blog post is 200–500 words, i.e. long enough to give you something of value but short enough to be digested in 5–10 minutes.

Unlike traditional printed newspapers and magazines, anyone can start a blog in minutes. There are many free blogging tools, e.g. WordPress (www.wordpress.com), Blogger (www.blogger.com) and Posterous (www.posterous.com) which will allow you to set up a free account in minutes and start blogging.

A blogger, i.e. the individual who maintains the blog, regularly updates the content on the site with short articles, i.e. blog posts. Most blogs are interactive, allowing visitors to comment on a blog post. Blogs can be anything from an online magazine with hundreds of thousands of regular readers, such as 'Mashable' (http://mashable.com), to an individual's online diary and personal journal which a few select friends and family are allowed to access.

It is this interactivity which enables blogging to be used as a networking tool. Chris Sherliker, managing partner of Silverman Sherliker LLP, maintains a blog – www.silvermansherlikerblog.com – and blogged about the pressures of legal practice in November 2009.[1] This was a subject near and dear to my own heart, and I left a lengthy comment about the impact of the chargeable time culture on the legal profession. This comment and subsequent discussion later led to me being invited to work with the firm extensively in 2010.

The point of a blog is to help people see past the commercial literature and help connect with you as a person, i.e. your personal brand – which is vital if you are to generate opportunities via your blogging activities. Your blog is a great tool to build up trust and credibility with your target audience, showing them you understand them, and know what you are talking about. In the world of online networking, your blog is your main asset to demonstrate your credibility with your target audience and strengthen your online personal brand.

What are the benefits of blogging?

A blog is a fantastic destination point to showcase your credibility to your target audience. When your target market 'meets' you in the online world,

[1] www.silvermansherlikerblog.com/developing-ninja-lawyer-skills

they are often interested to know whether you are the real deal or not. A well-maintained blog, which you direct people to read, whether via Twitter or a link on a forum post, is the easiest way to build up your credibility and strengthen your online personal brand.

Your page rank in Google is heavily influenced by how much fresh content you have on your website. As a blog is dynamic, i.e. users can interact with the website, Google is more likely to place a greater weight on a blog rather than a static website. This means that maintaining a keyword-rich blog is vital for effective search engine optimisation. Owning a website which features highly in the search engine ranking is a way of generating a ready-made interested audience to interact with, i.e. to network with you.

How to maximise your effectiveness with blogging

Similar to any kind of networking, to blog effectively you need to clarify why you are starting a blog and who you are writing it for. A well-written and thought-out blog will be a great source of credibility and strengthens your personal brand. A badly thought-out or written blog will be a drain on your time and reduce the impact of your personal brand, and damage your credibility.

Think about your target client. What sort of things will interest them? What problems or challenges do they face in their everyday lives? What do they read? What websites do they spend time surfing on?

Make sure you are always writing about subjects which are of value to your target audience, as this will encourage them to read, comment and return to your blog. Keeping a blog regularly updated takes time and effort, which is fine when you are light on client work. However, there will be times when you have some major client deadlines to meet and no spare time to blog. During the six months when I was focusing on writing this book, I used many guest blogs, i.e. blog posts written by someone other than me, to help keep my content fresh on all five of my blogs. Your blog doesn't always need to be written by you. Who else within your firm, team, department or network writes well and would be happy to write for your blog? There are many ghost bloggers who will write a blog post for you for a small fee!

Tip

Whenever you read a blog post which would be of value to your target audience, ask the blogger if you can republish it on your site, with full author credits. Unless they are a direct competitor of yours, most bloggers will say 'yes' and be genuinely flattered!

Using blogging as an effective networking tool is more than you solely pumping out content. The point of blogging, as a networking tool, is to connect with other people and to encourage people to read your blog. If you spend time commenting on other people's blogs, they will look at your blog and start to engage with your content. They may even ask you for a guest blog.

"They may even ask you for a guest blog"

An effective blog is visible to your target market. This means writing regular, fresh content and encouraging people within your online network to read your new content. Here are some suggestions of how to encourage people to read your blog:

- Post links on Twitter to newly written blogs.

- Include links to your blog post on your status update in LinkedIn and Facebook.

- Include a link to a blog post when you are answering a question in an online forum.

- Add a link to your blog in your email signature or forum signature.

Ten questions to help you improve the effectiveness of your blog

1 How will this post interest my target audience?

2 How will this post add value to my target audience?

3 Have you got a beginning, middle and end to your post?

4 Are you posting frequently enough for your target audience?

5 Is your post too long for the attention span of your target audience?

6 Have you got links into other websites and blogs (to improve your search engine optimisation)?

7 Are you putting important keywords into your post (to help your blog post get found)?

8 Does this post sound like me? (Or does my ghost blogger sound like me?)

9 How does this post link to my objectives for my blog?

10 Can I add a question to the end of my blog to encourage comments?

Many people ask the question, 'How often should I blog?' The right answer is based on how often your target audience expects to read your blog. For example, some bloggers blog a couple of times a day, but post up short sharp posts, and other bloggers write in-depth articles weekly. The right frequency will be based on the length, depth and breadth of your content, and what your target audience expects.

Eighteen ideas for what you can blog about

1   Book reviews
2   Presentations you have prepared
3   Proposals you have prepared
4   Video clips of you presenting at a seminar or conference
5   Lists of great websites or books that you think people should read
6   Anything that highlights your personal credentials
7   Any training events that you attend
8   Anything that occurs to you which may be of interest to your target audience
9   New products or services that you are starting to sell
10 Introductions to new team members
11 Case studies
12 Testimonials received from happy clients
13 Achievements of happy clients
14 What a client or you learned while working together
15 Interviews with experts inside and outside of your firm
16 Responses to news items or articles
17 Thought for the day
18 How-to articles

What do you need to include on your blog?

It's your blog, so unless you maintain it on behalf of your employers, you have total editorial freedom. However, this is what we recommend, as a minimum, you include on your blog:

▪ Contact details – how can people get in contact with you? Include both a telephone number and email address as different people prefer different ways of getting in touch.

▪ A page about you – include a professional-looking photograph and biography.

▪ A call to action – what do you want them to do as a result of reading your blog? Sign up for your mailing list?

▪ Links to your presence on social networking sites, e.g. Twitter, LinkedIn and Facebook.

▪ Links to your company's website.

The importance of your blog's title

People will take a decision to click through and read your blog based on its title. This means that the title of your blog is more important than the actual content of the blog. To influence a person to click through and actually read your blog post, a title needs to either promise value to the reader or pique their curiosity. A compelling title will help your article get noticed by an editor or guest blogger, who may request to use your content on their site.

Titles which help your blog post get more 'clicks' normally fall into the following categories:

- Clearly states what the post will deliver in the title, e.g. six tips to avoid stirring up trouble on social media.

- Promises to help people save money or time, e.g. simple ways all business owners can legally minimise their tax bill.

- Has a counter-intuitive title, for example, I once put this headline on my local branch's Chartered Institute of Personnel and Development (CIPD) newsletter: 'Why you shouldn't renew your CIPD membership'.

- 'Scares' your target market, e.g. 'Are you *legally* signing people up to your mailing list?'

- Includes your target audience's name in the title, e.g. 'Money laundering – what every business owner needs to know to keep them safe and legal'.

RSS feeds and feed readers

'RSS allows me to read all my favourite stuff in one place.'

Su Butcher, practice manager at Barefoot and Gilles

> **Tip**
>
> Sign up to Google Feedburner to get statistics of who has subscribed to your RSS feed, as well as offer your blog readers the opportunity to get your new blog posts automatically emailed to them.

RSS, which stands for Really Simple Syndication, is a way of reading frequently updated web pages such as blogs or news websites such as www. bbc.co.uk. An RSS feed reader – such as Google Reader – is a piece of software which allows you to access all your RSS feeds in one place.

Whenever you see the RSS icon shown below, this means that the website has the facility for you to add its feed to the feed reader of your choice.

For example, if you have three or four blogs which you like to read, you can add their RSS feed to your RSS feed reader, and whenever a new blog post is published, it will be placed in your RSS feed reader.

You want to be able to make it as easy as possible for people to regularly return to read your blog content. To help your readers do this, place an RSS icon in the top right-hand part of your blog layout. (Remember to link your blog feed's URL to the RSS icon.) Some people would prefer to have your new blog posts delivered straight to their inbox. A free service, such as Google Feedburner, will let you offer that facility to your blog readers.

Summary

A blog is a form of website where you can self-publish articles without needing the approval of anyone else. Anyone can start up a blog in minutes using a free blogging tool such as WordPress, Blogger or Posterous.

In the world of online networking, your blog is your main tool to demonstrate your credibility with your target audience and strengthen your online personal brand.

The point of a blog is to help people see past the commercial literature and help connect with you as a person.

A blog is an effective networking tool only if you have a mechanism for people to know about your blog and want to come and read it. An effective mechanism is to use online networking sites, such as Twitter or LinkedIn, to publicise your blog.

Use an RSS feed reader to access all your favourite blogs in one place. Include an RSS feed icon within your blog's layout to allow your readers to subscribe to your blog's RSS feed.

ACTION POINTS

■ Find three well-written blogs aimed at your target market and regularly read these blogs and comment on the blog posts.

■ Start your own blog or start contributing to your firm's blog.

■ Brainstorm with others potential subjects for your blog or your firm's blog.

■ Ask your clients which blogs they regularly read and what they would find of benefit in a blog.

■ Set up Google Feedburner for your blog, and put a 'subscribe to this blog' option – via either email or RSS feeder – in the top right-hand part of your blog's layout.

Further resources

Books

WordPress for Business Bloggers, Paul Thewlis, Packt Publishing, 2008.

ProBlogger: Secrets for blogging your way to a six-figure income, 2nd edition, Darren Rowse and Chris Garrett, John Wiley & Sons, 2010.

This Is Social Media: Blog, tweet, link your way to business success, Guy Clapperton, Capstone, 2009.

Me 2.0: Build a powerful brand to achieve career success, revised edition, Dan Schawbel, Kaplan Trade, 2010.

Social Media 101: Tactics and tips to develop your business online, Chris Brogan, John Wiley & Sons, 2010.

Websites and blogs

Joined up Business Networking www.joinedupnetworking.com

The Efficiency Coach on Business Efficiency http://business-efficiency. theefficiencycoach.co.uk

Blogging software

Wordpress wordpress.org and wordpress.com

Drupal www.drupal.org

Blogger www.blogger.com

Posterous www.posterous.com

part 3

Essential networking skills for the joined up networker

So far in the book we've looked at where to network, and the behaviours and attitudes needed to be a great networker. In the next part of the book, we are going to look at the skills needed when networking.

7

An introduction to the FITTER™ process for successful networking

What topics are covered in this chapter?

■ A simple networking model to help you network in a time-efficient manner

■ What research you can do to help you prepare for a networking event

■ How to categorise your network and focus your energy on the people who really matter to you

■ How you can follow up effectively after a networking event

'Networking takes a lot of your time and energy – and yet so many people simply go along and see what happens.'

Bryony Thomas, chief clear thinker at Clear Thought Consulting

Many professionals when networking have pleasant conversations, which lead precisely nowhere. Networking, without purpose, focus or results ends up being a massive waste of time and money. This is the reason I devised the FITTER™ model. I have developed the model over the past few years and used it to train professionals on how to network in a time-efficient manner. This model gives you a simple mnemonic which will enable you to network efficiently and effectively anywhere and any time.

What is the FITTER™ model?

The FITTER™ mnemonic is not a step-by-step process – you need to be mindful of doing *all* of these things *all* of the time when networking.

FITTER™ stands for:

Follow up
Introduce yourself with impact
Target specific people
Turn social conversations into business chat
Engage
Research

Follow up

'Similar to a golfer, the follow through for networkers, is as important as how you hit the ball.'

Jon Baker, partner at venture-now

How many times have you been along to a networking event and had some excellent conversations. Business cards are exchanged with a sincere desire to 'stay in touch'. You get back to work the next day, get stuck in with your client work; the people you met the day before soon become a distant memory and just another business card in the bottom of your drawer.

Does this sound familiar? Neglecting to follow up after a networking event is probably the biggest mistake professionals make when networking. Failing to follow up turns all your hard effort during the networking event into a waste of your time.

❝After an event, you need to sort the wood from the trees❞

Not everyone you meet will be important to you and your business or career going forward. After an event, you need to sort the wood from the trees, i.e. who is worth spending more time with to develop a stronger relationship.

> **Tip**
>
> Block out an hour in your diary the day after an event to follow up after a networking event.

After the event, within 24 hours of meeting someone, sort through the contacts you made and split them into three piles:

▧ *A-listers:* these are contacts who are well connected to your target market and are likely to help you immediately achieve your business or career goals, e.g. become a referral source, supplier, introducer or new client.

▧ *B-listers:* these are contacts you enjoyed meeting but are unlikely to immediately help you achieve your business or career goals.

▧ *C-listers:* these are contacts you met but are very unlikely to help you achieve your business or career goals.

> **Tip**
>
> Spend time with your team, agreeing on who or what makes up an A, B or C-lister for each person and the team as a whole. Agree on a process to introduce a new contact to the right member of the team.

Regardless of whether they are an A, B or C-lister, everyone needs to go into your contacts database, and ask to connect with them on Twitter. Even if you don't have specialist relationship management software, most email clients, such as Outlook and Google Contacts, will have the functionality to manage your contacts. Make a note of where you met them. Even if you don't think you'll get in touch, keep a note of the contact – you never know who people know!

> **Tip**
>
> To keep your A-listers visible, create a list for them in Twitter and a tag for them in your relationship management software and on LinkedIn.

When you add a contact, here are details that you should aim to record:

▧ name, address, telephone number(s)

▧ company name

▧ website address

▧ Twitter accounts – company and personal

▧ LinkedIn profile

- their company on LinkedIn

- note when and where you met. Additionally, jot some details about them and what you discussed

- add in some comment to help you remember them if you met them again – e.g. 'Looks a little bit like Sean Connery'.

When you are given someone's business card, always ask their permission to add them to your contact list and ask whether you might be able to send them an email or give them a ring. If you don't get their permission and you add them to your mailing list, you are violating anti-spamming laws in the US and the UK. If you have verbally gained permission to add a contact to your mailing list, then it is fine to add them when you return to the office.

When following up with your A and B-listers think about easy ways you can increase your social capital or credibility with them. For example:

- sending them an article which they will find interesting or useful

- offering to connect them to someone in your network

- sending them a link to a website or blog which will be useful to them.

Tip

If you have a long list of people you want to meet face-to-face, block out a day in your diary and aim to meet them on that day in a local hotel's lounge.

A-listers

Your A-list are people who will join the 'inner circle' of your network. These are the people who are most likely to help you achieve your networking objectives, e.g. finding a new business or a new job. After meeting an A-lister, you want to quickly strengthen the relationship, which means initiating a meeting – ideally in person, but otherwise via video call or phone call if a face-to-face meeting is not practical. Ideally, you would have already asked for a further conversation at the event; if not, pick up the phone or send an email, reminding them where you met them and indicating the benefit to them of spending more time with you.

For example:

> Hello Robert,
>
> It was great to meet you yesterday at the ICAEW event. I really enjoyed our conversation and would like to find out more about what you do with your clients in the manufacturing sector. That way, if I meet someone who needs your or your firm's services, I could recommend you to them.
>
> I'm happy to meet at a location of your choosing. However, there is a great little hotel, Harden Grange, near to the two of us where I tend to meet people. Coffee's on me! My diary is pretty free on Monday or Tuesday next week. Does either of those days work for you?
>
> My phone number is 0777 123 4567. Looking forward to getting to know you better.
>
> Kind regards,
>
> Brian

Tip

For the really important relationship, send a handwritten card or postcard rather than an email, saying how much you enjoyed meeting them. You'll be surprised how many people will keep the card displayed prominently on their desk.

On your relationship management system, set yourself up a recurring task to physically speak to your new A-lister at least once a month. Remember to send a request to connect with them on LinkedIn, stating where you met them. For example:

> Hello Robert,
>
> It was great to meet you yesterday at the ICAEW event. As you are a person I would value staying in touch with, I would like to add you to my LinkedIn contacts.
>
> Kind regards,
>
> Brian

'I always personalise my LinkedIn invitations, for example, 'It was great to talk to you yesterday', or 'Here is the article I promised I would send you'. This helps me be memorable and stand out from everyone else they met that day.'

Karen Spillane, training professional

B-listers

Your B-list are people who you want to stay in touch with but are unlikely in the short term to be a source of referrals, suppliers, introductions or new clients. However, you never know who they may meet, or what may change. Your aim is to connect with these people by as many touch points as possible, with minimal effort on your part.

> **Tip**
>
> To cut down the amount of time spent sending follow-up emails after an event, set up standard follow-up email templates for A, B and C-listers for you and others in your firm to use.

Similar to A-listers, connect with your B-listers on LinkedIn, and set yourself a recurring task to communicate with them at least once every three months. This could be an email, or message on Twitter or LinkedIn – it doesn't need to be a phone call or face-to-face meeting.

❝Connect with your B-listers on LinkedIn❞

Remember to send them a short email, within 48 hours of meeting them, stating how much you enjoyed meeting them and giving them a reason to sign up to your mailing list. For example:

Dear Juliet,

Hello, we met yesterday at the BNI's visitors' day.

I enjoyed our conversation and found your stories about the printing industry fascinating.

I would love to stay in touch, and have sent you a LinkedIn invite and started to follow you on Twitter (I'm @Sarah_James)

My firm sends out a monthly newsletter to everyone on our mailing list – full of interesting articles and advice for anyone wanting to minimise their tax bill. Anyone who signs up gets a copy of our firm's guide to future tax legislation and what it means for small businesses. If you would like a copy of this, then please click here to sign up to our mailing list.

If there is anything I can help you with, please give me a call.

Kind regards,

Sarah

C-listers

While C-listers are unlikely to be a useful contact for you, it is always worth generating a positive impression by sending them a follow-up email. After all, you never know who they may know. Very few people actually send follow up emails after an event, and this small act will boost your social capital and credibility. For example:

Dear Juliet,

Hello, we met yesterday at the BNI's visitor's day.

It was good to talk to you, and good luck with your future plans. I've started to follow you on Twitter. (I'm @Sarah_James)

Just in case you know anyone who may be interested, my firm sends out a monthly newsletter to everyone on our mailing list – full of interesting articles and advice for anyone wanting to minimise their tax bill. Anyone who signs up gets a copy of our firm's guide to future tax legislation and what it means for small businesses. If you know someone who would benefit from a copy of this, then please forward on this email to them. They will need to <u>click here</u> to sign up to our mailing list.

If there is anything I can help you with, please give me a call.

Kind regards,

Sarah

Introduce yourself with impact

You only ever get one chance to make a great first impression. So it's important to introduce yourself with impact – one which will highlight your credibility and encourage people to engage with you. In Chapter 8 you will discover how to make the right first impression and what to say when asked the question, '*So, what do you do?*'

Target specific people

If you've ever been to a networking event, you will know how easy it is to end up having great conversations but not actually talking to the people you have gone to the event to meet. If you have done your homework before an event (see the later section in this chapter on research), you will have a short list of five to ten people you want to meet at the event. How many of these people could you contact via LinkedIn beforehand and arrange to meet at the event? Perhaps you could get your host to introduce you to them?

'I want to maximise my effectiveness when networking, so I will only sign up for an event when I know that at least three people I want to meet will be there.'

Jay Blake, director at Ichthus Video[1]

Before you attend an event, tweet that you are attending and use your LinkedIn status to let people know you are going, asking whether anyone else is also going. This may encourage someone who wants to meet you or get to know you better to attend the same event. When I tweeted that I was going to attend the tweetup after the Lex 2011 conference at least two people decided to attend just to meet me. Connecting up with people in advance of an event gives you additional purpose to attend the event, as well as the opportunity to strengthen an existing relationship. If you don't already know someone you are meeting, agree a time and location to meet – for example, by the event registration stand.

For more details on how to target specific people, see Chapter 10, 'How to work a room'.

Turn social conversations into business chat

'Don't count conversations, make your conversations count.'

Rob Brown, motivational speaker and networking expert[2]

If you've done your research, you will know what you ideally want to achieve as a result of meeting this person. However, do not fall into the trap of diving straight into business. Blurting out your objective for meeting someone within the first minute of meeting them is very unlikely to be constructive. Before you start talking business, take your time to get to know the person and generate some rapport. See Chapter 9 for more detail on how to quickly generate rapport with everyone.

Some good questions to use to move your conversation into a business-orientated conversation include:

■ How's business at the moment?

■ What's your ideal client?

■ What problems do you solve for your clients?

■ How do you market your business?

■ What challenges are you facing at the moment?

■ Who is your ideal referral source?

---

[1] www.ichthusvideo.co.uk

[2] www.rob-brown.com

Engage

When meeting someone at a networking event, focus 80 per cent of your energy on listening and finding out about them: their objectives for being at the event, who they are, shared hobbies, interests and mutual acquaintances, and what makes them tick. Remember, you are not there to sell; you are there to start a mutually beneficial relationship, which can be accelerated by being able to help them there and then.

❝You are there to start a mutually beneficial relationship❞

For example, how about asking them:

■ What has brought them to this event?

■ Who are they hoping to meet at the event?

■ What do they want to achieve by the end of the event?

Most people, unless they are very self-obsessed, will always reciprocate and find out about you and your agenda. If they don't, do you really want to spend time on someone who is not interested in you?

For more details on how to engage in a conversation, see Chapter 8, 'Making the right first impression' and Chapter 10, 'How to work a room'.

Research

Before you attend a networking event, you need to do your homework. Your research will enable you to focus only on the events worth attending, the people who will be beneficial to you to meet or re-connect with and good topics to talk about. This research can be done for you by your personal assistant. Let's say you are an accountant and are looking for a new job within a private practice locally. Therefore, you want to be meeting partners within local accountancy firms and people well connected to these firms, e.g. partners within law firms. Your research will identify which local events they are likely to turn up to, plus who are the people from the firm you would benefit from an introduction to.

Tip

Use an RSS reader, such as Google Reader, to take a feed from websites of organisations which host events you may want to attend. This way you will be automatically informed of good events for you to attend.

Once you know what event you are going to attend, the next stage is to prioritise who you want to meet. Most event organisers will give you a delegate list in advance. See if the event is listed on LinkedIn or Facebook, and see who has listed themselves as going. If you are on Twitter, tweet that you are going and ask if anyone else is.

> ### Tip
>
> Don't forget to re-connect with existing members of your network at events. Strengthening your network is just as important as extending your network.

After you have a list of people attending the event, it is time to find out as much as you can about the attendees, and crucially what they look like. Your aim is to have a short list of about five to ten people who you would really like to meet.

Here's how you can find out more about someone:

■ Search for them on LinkedIn.

■ Look at their company website.

■ Do a Google search on their name.

■ Search for them on Facebook.

■ See whether any of your trusted connections on LinkedIn are connected to them and could tell you more about them.

■ See whether they are on Twitter and what they tweet about.

Remember that your aim is to find five to ten target people, and something that you can ask them which gets them talking to you. It's a great way to make a first impression and quickly build rapport and credibility if you can demonstrate some shared knowledge or connection.

'Hello Lola, I was hoping to meet you here tonight. I think we have a mutual friend in Dwain. May I ask how you met him?'

Spend some time thinking what you would like to achieve as a result of meeting these people. Is it a further meeting, an introduction to someone in their organisation, or a chance to send them an article or white paper?

Either on the day before the event or the morning of the event, have a quick scan through the news, business and sports sections of the BBC website and industry-related press. This will give you conversation starters at the event and an opportunity to voice your opinion and demonstrate your professional credibility.

Summary

FITTER™ stands for:

Follow up: sort people into A, B and C-listers, add them into your database and make contact with them.

Introduce yourself with impact: a good impression will start a mutually good relationship.

Target specific people: your time is precious, so make sure you know who you want to meet and why you want to meet them.

Turn social conversations into business chat: take your time to get to know the person first and then move the conversation on to business topics.

Engage: focus 80 per cent of your energy on listening and finding out about them.

Research: focus only on events worth attending and the people worth meeting.

ACTION POINTS

■ Think about your current business or career objectives. What defines, for you personally, an A, B or C-lister? What questions can you ask to help you identify A-listers?

■ Look at your current network. Who are your A-listers? How many of them have you spoken to in the last month? How could you strengthen your relationships with your A-listers?

■ If you already have a contacts database for your network, add in an extra column or field where you can categorise your existing contacts as A, B or C-listers. Then review all your existing contacts.

■ Where could you network to start meeting A or B-listers?

■ What preparation do you complete before you attend a networking event? What could you do to better prepare before you attend an event?

■ Before your next networking event, identify a shortlist of five to ten people you want to meet. What can you find out about them using Google, LinkedIn and Twitter?

■ What processes and systems can you put in place to consistently follow up both with new people you meet and your existing network?

Further resources

Books

Never Eat Alone: And other secrets to success, one relationship at a time, 2nd edition, Keith Ferrazzi, Doubleday, 2011.

The Tipping Point, Malcolm Gladwell, Abacus, 2001.

Websites and blogs

Joined Up Networking www.joinedupnetworking.com

Winning business – the secrets of staying in touch www.winningbusiness.net/downloads/pdfs/InTouch.pdf

8

Making the right first impression

What topics are covered in this chapter?

- How to introduce yourself with impact
- What to put into your 60 second pitch for maximum success
- How to present your best online 'face'

In the last chapter we explored how you can use the FITTER™ model to network efficiently and effectively anywhere and any time. Up to this point in the book, we have been talking about the behaviours, attitudes and ingredients necessary to be successful as a networker. Underpinning these success factors is a networker's ability to make the right first impression. Without a great first impression, the relationship is going to struggle to start. In this chapter we will look at how to make a great and memorable first impression.

How to make the right first impression when meeting people

First impressions are everything. Get it right and everything becomes easy. Get it wrong and you have a hard task ahead of you to correct those all-important first impressions. We humans can't help forming an opinion in a few seconds when we meet a stranger; it's how we are programmed for survival.

So, what do I mean by a great first impression? In both the real and virtual world people respond well to warm, positive and confident folk. If you are

❝People respond well to warm, positive and confident folk❞

meeting someone in person, this means offer your handshake first, give them a warm smile and be positive and enthusiastic. This simple act will convey credibility and a likeable personal brand.

If someone is meeting you for the first time in the virtual world, there isn't the equivalent of a handshake. But don't be fooled, they will still be forming a perception of you from that first meeting. If your answer, tweet or blog post conveys warmth, positivity, authenticity and likeability, then you are halfway there to creating a great first impression. If your first online meeting is positive, the next thing that someone will do is look at your profile, blog or website. This is why it is so important to spend time on your social networking profiles and general web presence.

The importance of your handshake

What's worse? A palm-shattering, bone crunching handshake? Or being offered a hand which feels more like a limp fish? Originally handshakes were used to prove that we came in peace and did not have a weapon. Nowadays, we use handshakes all the time – but particularly when meeting and greeting someone.

Handshakes are a sign of trust and help build strong relationships. Your handshake is just one of the ways you can build a positive first impression. Psychologists have found that if you take the initiative and move forward to meet a person and shake their hand, their impression of you will be more favourable than if you waited for them to make the initiative.

However, handshakes mean different things in different cultures. In today's global marketplace, you could find yourself networking with people from Africa, Japan or the US. Whereas in the US a firm handshake equals self-confidence, in Africa a limp handshake is the way to do it. In Africa, expect to be shaking hands for as much as a couple of minutes. In the US, expect to get some very strange looks if your handshake goes on for more than a few seconds.

I'm guessing that many people don't know the full impact of their handshake – and don't even give their handshake a moment's thought. My suggestion is you need to be aware of the first impression that your handshake portrays. That's right, I'm suggesting that you practise your handshake on people you trust. Sounds embarrassing? It is far better to identify and fix a problem handshake before it impacts on your career or potential to win new business.

Dress for success

How do I put this delicately? Appearances do count, and stereotypes do exist. If you think of a lawyer, you expect to see a well-tailored suit and a neat appearance. As many image consultant will tell you, details are important. Chipped nail polish or dirty nails is a no-no, as is missing buttons from a coat, dirty shoes or messy hair. To give you an analogy, would you return to a shop if it had dirty carpets and dust on the shelf?

If you look good and have a confident handshake, then the battle for the right first impression is nearly won.

Your opening sound bite

The last piece of the jigsaw is how you introduce yourself. For many professionals, a big trap is waiting for them when asked (the almost standard question at a networking event), 'So what do you do?' Do you confess and say, I'm an accountant … lawyer … coach …? Or do you describe what you do by the value you bring to your clients? For example, an accountant may describe what they do like this:

'I help my clients legally pay only the right amount of tax, not a penny more, not a penny less.'

The right answer is to have the one-sentence sound bite prepared, which succinctly talks about the value you bring to your clients. This is my opening sound bite: *'I help professionals gain better business results for less effort.'* By talking about the value you bring to your clients early in the conversation, you are emphasising the benefits of your service rather than the features. After all, every sales person will tell you that people buy benefits, not features.

When I train people to use an opening sound bite describing the value they bring to their clients, many worry that the other person won't know what they do. I can see that this is a genuine concern. However, in my experience, whenever this type of opening is used, the next question is, 'Oh, that sounds interesting, how do you do that?' And then you are off, the conversation is started, and you have moved straight into a business conversation.

A networker's pitch

Attend any referral generation club, e.g. a 4Networking breakfast meeting, or speed networking event and everyone will be asked to deliver a pitch on behalf of their business. Often this pitch will be the first time that all of the club members have met you. There are many reasons why your pitch needs to be word perfect – and we will discuss these in this chapter – however, your pitch is a point in time when people will be forming a first impression of you. Typically, most networking events limit people's pitches to one minute or less, which is why they are often called 60-second pitches. A well-delivered and thought-out pitch will encourage club members to help you and interact with you.

❝These pitches are your opportunity to talk about your business❞

In essence, these pitches are your opportunity to talk about your business and ask the other people at the meeting for help to achieve your networking objectives. Your networking pitch is the only time when networking that you are allowed to sell!

A successful pitch has the following characteristics:

- Short and punchy and keeps strictly to the time limit.
- Engages the audience by starting with a question.
- Is specific in who or what help you want from the group, i.e. a call to action.
- Demonstrates your credibility.
- Talks about only one feature of your service.
- Repeats your name twice with features of your service, as it helps people to remember you.
- Is memorable.

'I use a large plastic funnel to emphasise during my 60-second pitch how the use of video can help our clients at each stage of the marketing and sales funnel to convert prospects into new business.'

Jay Blake, managing director of Ichthus Video

What should go into your pitch?

Your aim with a pitch is to encourage people to take action and think about whom within their networks can help you. You will often hear this in networking circles called 'selling through the room' rather than 'selling to the room'. If there are ten people in the room listening to your pitch, and each of them has a good network of more than 100 people, then if you 'sell through the room', i.e. to each of their networks, rather than to each of the people in the room directly, you have a greater probability of success.

> **Tip**
>
> Plan your pitch in advance and in conjunction with your marketing plan.

In the FITTER™ model we talked about targeting specific people. When preparing your pitch you need to first think about what you are trying to achieve by being at that networking event, e.g. who are you looking to meet? The more specific you are on who you want to meet, the more quality introductions and referrals you will receive. Perhaps more importantly, who are you representing? Some networkers have several business interests and need to decide, when they are out networking, which business they are representing. Sixty seconds is too short to try to 'pitch' two businesses – it will only confuse the audience. For example, there will be times when I want to actively push my role as chief coach at The Efficiency Coach, but other times when I want to be known as the co-founder of The Executive Village. Before I go to an event where I will have to deliver a 60-second pitch, I will decide which of my two businesses I am promoting to the event.

> **Tip**
>
> Think about using a prop, e.g. a picture, for your pitch. It will help to make you more memorable.

Next, think about what client pain you solve with your services. What example can you think of to highlight your credibility at solving your client's problems, e.g. a client testimonial or recent case study? Include evidence of the benefits your product or service brought to your client.

> **Tip**
>
> To help calm your nerves before delivering your pitch, visualise yourself delivering the pitch perfectly, with everyone listening intently.

Here is a simple structure for you to use to put together your pitch:

1 Say your name, the name of your company and the value you bring to your clients, which is a question rather than a statement. E.g.

Hello, my name is Heather Townsend and I am the chief coach at The Efficiency Coach. Would you like to be able to gain 20 per cent better business results for less effort?

2 Then who you work with:

We work exclusively with professional advisors, such as lawyers and accountants.

3 Then talk about something that demonstrates your credibility:

I've been coaching a partner who has just left one of the big four accountancy practices after 30 years of service. He hired me to consider what he should do with his career going forward. After just two sessions working together, he told me, 'Thanks to your coaching, I now know where I want to take my career and have stopped dreaming about life back in my old firm. I would have paid millions to stop having those dreams.'

4 What you are looking for:

This week I am looking for lawyers and accountants whose practice is growing rapidly and are stressed with their ever growing workload. Who do you know who fits this description?

5 Repeat your name and your business:

I'm Heather Townsend, the chief coach at The Efficiency Coach. Who would like to be able to gain better 20 per cent business results for less effort?

> **Tip**
>
> Keep the messages of your pitch consistent but vary the content of your pitch, so your regular audience has a reason to listen to your pitch week in week out.

Many well-attended referral generation clubs will let members have only 40 seconds for their pitch. For example, this is the short pitch which Paula Jones, managing director of 6th Level Training, uses:

'My name is Paula and I am the managing director of 6th Level Training. Do you have enough hours in the day? Would you like to be able to gain back up to two hours a day? If that sounds like something which would be useful to you or someone you know then ask to have a 1:2:1 with me about our time-management training.

We are looking for small businesses which are looking to increase their efficiency, by helping their staff use their time more productively.

I am Paula Jones, the managing director of 6th Level Training, and looking for decision makers in small businesses who are looking to help their staff improve their time management.'

> **Tip**
>
> When you are new to a referral generation club, use your pitch to showcase your credibility and build up trust rather than ask for business.

In my earlier example, I used a client testimonial in my pitch to establish my credibility with the audience. There are many different ways to establish your credibility in your pitch, for example:

- Talk about what you have achieved for your clients in the last few weeks.
- Describe how you went the extra mile for a client.
- Mention new client wins and why they chose you.
- Chat about any recent PR, award wins or good stuff that has happened.
- Speak with confidence, as your audience is wanting to see that you are confident in your product or service and you can deliver to time and the right level of quality.
- Keep your message consistent.

Your online footprint

> **Tip**
>
> When writing your profile in Twitter, include the people you would like to follow you. Many people use search tools to find people with certain words in their profile.

The online equivalent of a networking pitch and opening sound bite is your online profile or biography. When someone connects with you online and likes what they see, the first thing they normally read is your profile or online biography. Their reason? It's to find out more about you and evaluate whether you are the type of person they want to get to know. This may sound callous, but every time you meet someone new in person, you are subconsciously deciding whether you want to get to know them better. This may only be the quick decision whether to follow someone on Twitter, or it may be a decision to contact them with a view to hiring them in the future.

> **Tip**
>
> Use a professionally taken head-and-shoulders shot of yourself for your online picture. Don't use your company's logo, as people want to meet you, not your company.

Your online presence needs to include a professional head-and-shoulders shot of you, demonstrate your credibility and position your brand, e.g. state who you work with, and the problems which you solve for your clients. Very often a social networking site, e.g. LinkedIn, and the profiles within it are rated very highly by Google. Therefore, to help you appear near the top of the search engine rankings for content you control, it is important to include keywords in your profile which your clients are likely to be searching for online.

❝It is important to include keywords in your profile❞

> **Tip**
>
> To keep your private life truly private on Facebook, untag yourself from incriminating photos and set your privacy settings to the highest level.

When we meet someone in person, very often our instinct tells us whether we can trust them or not. When we meet someone online, we can only rely on the written word and what their photo looks like. Trust is often generated in online relationships by consistency, i.e. answering the same types of questions, tweeting on similar themes and having the same profile and professional-looking photo, regardless of which online networking site you meet people on.

What needs to go in your online biography or profile

Your online biography or 'bio' is part of your networking toolkit. You need to have a couple of versions of your online biography prepared, for example:

- to use as an author credit for your articles
- to use within marketing materials, for example if you are a guest speaker
- in your social networking site's profiles, e.g. Twitter and LinkedIn.

> **Tip**
>
> Ask your photographer to supply you with both high- and low-resolution versions of your professional head-and-shoulders photo. The high-resolution version should be supplied for printed materials and the low-resolution version to be used online.

Your basic biography needs to consist of your professional head-and-shoulders photo, one sentence stating what you do, then a paragraph qualifying your credibility. For example, here is my basic biography.

My one sentence stating what I do:
Heather Townsend is a widely published author, performance improvement specialist to professional service firms, and social media expert.

My paragraph qualifying my credibility:

Heather, in the last decade, has worked with over one hundred partners, coached and trained over 1000 lawyers, accountants and other professionals at every level, in the UK's top and most ambitious professional practices. She is the UK's foremost expert on how business people can build meaningful and profitable relationships via social media. She has been commissioned to write on key business topics by the Financial Times. *Heather is the founder and chief coach at The Efficiency Coach, and co-founder of The Executive Village.*

Some tips when writing your basic biography:

- Keep it short and sweet, less is more.
- Don't claim to be more than three things, as it damages your credibility.
- Include links back to your website and blog.
- For social networking profiles, especially LinkedIn, include keywords within your profile.

Summary

First impressions are everything. Get it right, and everything becomes easy. When answering the question 'So what do you do?', always answer with the value you bring to your clients, not your occupation or job title.

At a formal networking event, it is vital to prepare a short, punchy but well-thought-out pitch.

Your aim with a pitch is to establish your credibility, be memorable and encourage people to think about who within their networks can help you.

Your online profile needs to be as professional as your personal presence in a networking meeting.

Prepare several versions of your online biography, which state what you do and qualify your credibility.

ACTION POINTS

▨ Ask for feedback on your normal handshake – does it convey the right first impression? Practise on a friend until you get it right.

▨ Next time you are out at a networking event, aim to be the person who initiates a conversation and leans forward to shake hands. Notice how you are treated differently when doing this.

▨ Write out your opening sound bite by describing in one sentence the value you (or your business) bring to your clients. Test out this sound bite next time you are meeting new people at a networking event.

▨ Look at your company's marketing plan. How can you use your networking pitch to help make your company's marketing campaigns a success?

▨ Watch an established networker deliver their pitch. What do they do well? What can you copy?

▨ What props could you use to strengthen your impact next time you deliver your pitch?

▨ Before you attend your next networking event, take the time to practise your pitch before you deliver it. How does this help improve your impact at the event?

▨ Ask for some feedback on your pitch next time you deliver it. Find out what you can do to improve your impact.

▨ Ask for some feedback on your professional photo which you use on your social networking profiles. Do you look open, warm and welcoming?

▨ If you don't have a professional photo on your online profiles, organise a photo shoot with a professional photographer.

▨ Write your basic online biography, and keep it to one sentence describing what you do, then one short paragraph qualifying your credibility and expertise.

▨ Read your online profiles and biographies – critique them for consistency and credibility. If you don't feel confident in your writing abilities, how about hiring a copywriter to write them for you?

Further resources

Books

Networking Like A Pro: Turning contacts into connections, Ivan R. Misner, David C. Alexander and Brian Hilliard, Entrepreneur Press, 2010.

Confident Networking for Career Success and Satisfaction, Gael Lindenfield and Stuart Lindenfield, Piatkus Books, 2005.

Brilliant Networking: What the best networkers, know, do and say, 2nd edition, Stephen D'Souza, Prentice Hall, 2010.

Me 2.0: Build a powerful brand to achieve career success, revised edition, Dan Schawbel, Kaplan Trade, 2010.

Blogs and website

Joined Up Business Networking www.joinedupnetworking.com

Dan Schawbel's personal branding blog www.personalbrandingblog.com

9

How to keep the conversation going

What topics are covered in this chapter?

- How to generate rapport with anyone you meet
- How to recognise the three different communication styles: think, feel, know
- How to have a productive conversation with everyone you meet

In the last chapter we showed you how to make that all-important first impression. But then what happens? How do you go from meeting someone to building a relationship? A connection becomes a positive relationship only when the two of you have rapport and the conversation flows easily. In this chapter we introduce the three different communication styles: think, feel and know. Using these, you can flex your personal style to quickly recognise and build rapport with people with different styles, regardless of whether you are meeting them in person, virtually or via a phone/video call.

What do we mean by rapport?

People like people who are like themselves or who behave like them. Sensing that someone else is like you is done at the conscious and subconscious (or unconscious) level. Two people who sense that each is like the other at an unconscious level are said to be 'in rapport'. Having an awareness of the conditions needed to generate rapport enables you to adjust your personal style to consciously build rapport with everyone you meet. Ultimately, it is how you choose to communicate that informs the subconscious decision of whether someone will like you or not.

> **Tip**
>
> When you meet someone for the first time, find something that you can sincerely compliment them on.

❝Mirroring naturally happens when you have generated rapport❞

Many textbooks and training workshops will teach you a technique called mirroring. This is where you copy the other person's body language, to try to build rapport. While this sounds fine in theory, in practice it never works. In fact, mirroring naturally happens when you have generated rapport, rather than rapport being generated because you have copied someone's gestures.

case study Hamish Taylor

Hamish Taylor was leading a team from ICI who were meeting with a team from Procter & Gamble to investigate ways of sharing and collaborating on innovative products and technologies. Before the meeting Hamish had looked up every Procter & Gamble-er and identified what their particular expertise and interests were. He used this information to tailor parts of his presentation to connect with each individual member of the Procter & Gamble team's personal agendas. Unsurprisingly, this research was instrumental in setting the stage for a productive meeting.

During the meeting, Hamish overheard a senior Procter & Gamble executive remark, 'I've never met or heard of this Hamish guy before.' Upon hearing this, Hamish quickly re-read the dossier he had compiled on him as an individual. When an occasion presented itself, Hamish took the opportunity to talk with the senior executive. After a few minutes of small talk, Hamish started talking about his time in Japan and how much he had admired the way that Procter & Gamble had dealt with the aftermath of the Kobe earthquake. This was no chance remark, as Hamish knew that this person had been the one directly 'shaken up' by that earthquake. This shared interest, and subsequent conversation, led to a very strong friendship and mutually beneficial relationship between the two of them.

It was the rapid establishment of rapport, as well as the depth of rapport, which led to strong ties between the two teams. The subsequent joint collaboration between the two teams enabled Hamish's subsidiary of ICI's business with Procter & Gamble to grow from $10m to $70m in less than five years.

How do people choose to communicate?

Picture the scenario of two people meeting at a networking event. One person asks the other,

'So, what do you do?'

There are three different styles of response:

1 The other person replies with thoughtful, paced and structured detail about what they actually do. For example:

'I do three things. Firstly I am a holistic financial planner for my company, Safe Financial Services. This takes up all my working time. I'm also a husband and father to my two children, Aggie and James, and once a week I volunteer at my local church.'

2 The other person is ready to unburden everything they do. They seem to go on and on, with high amounts of energy, lots of stories and animated gestures. For example:

'I love what I do! One of my clients described me the other day as a 'money-saver', but another client recently described me as 'guardian of his finances'. I personally always get a real buzz when I can see a client who I signed up, achieving their financial goals. I don't feel as if I am a financial advisor, as that sounds rather boring ...'

3 The other person answers in a succinct, straightforward, calm way, often using only one word or one sentence. For example:

'I'm a financial advisor for Safe Financial Services.'

Each of these three different responses is sending a signal about how the person prefers to be communicated with. These three responses are typical of the three different communication styles.

Response	Style	Attuned to:
1	Think	Data
2	Feel	Energy
3	Know	Gut instinct

The three different communication styles

People communicate information based on the way we use the three innate communication styles of *thinking*, *feeling* and *knowing*. There is no one style which is better than another. We can all use all three styles, but we tend to have a preference for one or two styles.

Your aim as a networker is to be able to have a meaningful conversation with every person you meet, and to strengthen the relationship between the two of you. If you meet someone who shares the same communication style preference as yourself, then rapport will naturally develop; however, there is no guarantee that you will have a productive conversation.

I personally have an equally strong preference for 'feel' and 'know'. However, it depends on who I am with, where I am and how I am feeling at the time whether the 'feel' or the 'know' will dominate my communication style. If you can spot someone's natural preference for a communication style, by adapting your style to theirs you will reduce miscommunication and promote rapport. In written communication, such as emails, blogs, online forms, your connection and relationship will be improved if you adapt to the primary preference of your target.

Think

People with a preference for 'think' like to receive data, absorb all the details and process information in a methodical and logical way. They like to have all the facts before acting.

❝People with a preference for 'think' like to receive data❞

Thinking communication tends to be in the form of numbers, data and facts. It comprises lengthy processes of thinking through issues. Typically, every step and thought is shared.

If you asked someone with a primary 'think' communication preference *'So, how's business?'*, they would tend to respond something like this: *'I need to tell you seven things about my business (Pause for thought)...'* and whether you like it or not, they will tell you in whole paragraphs what those seven points are.

To build rapport with a 'think' communication style

Use whole paragraphs, structures, logic, detail.

To have a productive conversation with someone who has a 'think' preference

When you meet someone with a 'think' preference, they will often appear thoughtful and will be very structured and detailed. If you don't have a 'think' preference, the level of detail being communicated can seem inconsequential and boring. Someone with a 'know' preference will soon get frustrated when communicating with a 'think' preference, as it will feel as if they don't get to the point, or even worse don't appear to listen to you.

To build the relationship and keep a meaningful conversation flowing:

- Put structure into your conversation, e.g.
  'There are three things I'm going to tell you about my business. I will tell you about the background of the business, the services we offer, and some recent success stories from our clients.'
- Ask at the beginning of the conversation what they want to get out of the conversation
- Signpost your intentions, e.g.
  'I would love to spend 5–10 minutes finding out more about you and your business.'
- Ask what it would be helpful for them to know about you and your business.
- Summarise regularly for them
- Be patient and let them get the detail out

Feel

People with a preference for 'feel' are attuned to other people's energy and consider this before making decisions. They empathise with others and are sensitive to their moods. They tend to communicate in stories. They will use visual language, analogies, colours and verbs.

Feeling communication relates how an individual 'feels' in or about a situation. The best example of this is walking into a meeting where you can almost 'cut the air with a knife' – this is a feeling.

If you ask someone with a 'feel' preference at a networking event, *'So, how's business?'*, they are likely to respond in two different ways – depending on whether they are having a good day or a bad day.

'Everything's fantastic, amazing, a little bit frantic – let me paint a picture of my day for you – and let me tell you how I helped my client this week,' accompanied by an animated face and lots of hand gestures.

Or,

'Business is pretty pants at the moment, and I don't know why I keep on trying to push water uphill with a sieve. If I'm honest I don't know why I came out tonight.'

To build rapport with a 'feel' communication style

Summarise and show empathy, and aim to relate to the other person's underlying meanings and motivation.

To have a productive conversation with someone who has a 'feel' communication style

When you meet someone with a 'feel' preference, they tend to have a lot to say. Their emotions are always near to the surface, and normally you are left in no doubt as to what they feel about something. To someone with a 'think' or a 'know' preference, someone with a 'feel' preference can seem disjointed and go off on tangents. If someone with a 'feel' preference is nervous, the stories may seem to be told for stories' sake. Keeping a conversation going with someone with a 'feel' preference is never hard – but getting a word in edgeways or keeping the conversation focused may not be easy!

> **❝ Keeping a conversation going with someone with a 'feel' preference is never hard ❞**

If you meet someone with a 'feel' preference, to keep the conversation flowing and build the relationship:

- Summarise what they are saying.
- Use stories, analogies and metaphors.
- Search for common values, interests and motivations – people with a 'feel' communication preference need to feel a connection.

■ Keep the conversation focused, and if necessary interrupt to bring them back 'on topic'.

Know

People with a preference for 'know' take a position and make decisions quickly. They are sometimes unable to explain that decision, which is based on their gut instinct. Very often their answers to questions will be short and succinct.

Knowing communication is instinctive. 'Know' preferences can come across in a harsh manner at times, especially to people with 'feel' and 'think' preferences, who prefer to express themselves with more words and description.

If you ask someone with a 'know' preference at a networking event, *'So, how's business?', they* are likely to respond:

'Good – keeping busy.'

To build rapport with a 'know' communication style

Use short sentences and questions encouraging them to elaborate. Always get to the point quickly, and be succinct.

To have a productive conversation with someone who has a 'know' communication style

These people can be very self-contained and relationship-building behaviours, for example indulging in small talk, may not always be apparent. This self-containment coupled with a potential lack of relationship-building conversations can make someone with a strong 'know' preference come across as rude and arrogant. The challenge when you meet someone with an apparent 'know' preference is to keep the conversation going and get them to elaborate enough to find areas of shared interest. Unlike people with a 'feel' preference, people with a 'know' preference are often happy to sit in silence. When you meet someone with a 'know' preference you may come away from the conversation feeling that you haven't connected – but persevere, as the person with a strong preference for 'know', as opposed to someone with a strong 'think' or 'feel' preference, can take longer to bond with others.

Tip

If you have met someone and the conversation is not flowing, even though you think you are asking the right questions, there is a strong likelihood that they have a preference for 'know'.

If you meet someone with a 'know' preference, to keep the conversation flowing and build the relationship:

■ Ask open questions which extract details, e.g.
  'What are you looking to get out of the event today?'
  'What does your business do?'
  'Was there anyone here you particularly wanted to meet? If so, why?'

■ Keep the conversation focused – don't ramble and keep to the point.

■ Don't worry if there is an occasional silence or pause in the conversation.

■ Check in regularly with them that the conversation is beneficial for them.

The ThinkFeelKnow© indicator

If you are interested in finding out what your natural communication style is or helping your team to understand their natural communication styles, there is an easy-to-complete ThinkFeelKnow© indicator profiling tool. This tool provides a personalised online report for people profiling their preferences for the three communication styles. The ThinkFeelKnow© indicator can be accessed via www.thinkfeelknow.com.

exercise

Think about five people you work closely with, and using your knowledge about the ThinkFeelKnow© indicator, identify what you think is their natural communication style. Is it think, feel or know? When you next meet them, change your normal style of communication to match theirs and see what changes as a result.

How to find areas of common interest

❝You need to start with small talk❞

Every productive conversation needs to start somewhere. First, you need to find someone to talk to, then you have to get the conversation going. Before you can take a conversation so that it becomes a meaningful experience, you need to start with small talk. Joining people in the queue for food or the bar is a great way to start small talk with someone. It's easy to comment on something to do with the situation you are in, for example:

'The food looks fantastic tonight.'
'Bang goes my diet for today!'
'What takes your fancy on the menu this lunchtime?'
'I'm looking forward to a cold drink. What are you having?'

The purpose of small talk in this instance is to safely get the conversation started. Good positions to stand where you won't be short of someone to talk to are:

■ near the drinks table

■ by the seating plan

■ near the entrance.

If you don't fancy waiting until someone comes to find you, all you need to do is catch someone's eye and smile at them. I promise you, they will come over and talk to you.

While speaking to random people at networking events is all part of the fun of networking, it pays to share your goals early with the people you are meeting – particularly with people who have a 'know' communication preference. This way, you will find out quickly how much time you should invest in the conversation. These questions can help you safely share your personal objectives for the event:

'What are you looking to achieve here today?'
'What made you decide to come to this conference?'

Good questions to keep the conversation going

■ What prompted you to become a …?

■ How's business?

■ What's your ideal client?

■ What does the future hold for you/your business?

■ What have you been enjoying watching recently on TV?

■ What are your interests outside of work?

■ Have you always lived around here?

■ What prompted you to set up your own business?

■ What are you enjoying listening to/watching at the moment?

■ What sports do you enjoy watching or playing?

Summary

By generating rapport, you are on your way to establishing a mutually beneficial relationship.

There are three communication styles: think, feel, know. To build rapport, you need to learn how to spot the style of other people and then interact with them in a similar style.

Think	Thoughtful, precise, paragraphs, lots of words, numbers
Feel	High energy, passion, visual language, colours, verbs, stories, analogies
Know	Self-contained, calm, headings, short sharp answers – 'bullet points'

Your aim once you have introduced yourself is to generate a conversation where you can explore and identify areas of common interest and value.

ACTION POINTS

■ Next time you are out working the room, aim to see whether you can find business or personal contacts you have in common with someone. Notice how the level of rapport changes between the two of you when you have established a mutual contact.

■ Identify your communication style preference by completing the ThinkFeelKnow© indicator at www.thinkfeelknow.com

■ Think about your close circle of friends – who has a preference for 'think', 'feel' and 'know'?

■ Find someone you know with a different communication preference to you. Have a go at adapting your style to match theirs. Observe how the conversation flows more freely between the two of you.

Further resources

Books

Perfect Phrases for Professional Networking, Susan Benjamin, McGraw-Hill Professional, 2009.

Brilliant Networking: What the best networkers know, do and say, 2nd edition, Stephen D'Souza, Prentice Hall, 2010.

Blogs and websites

Joined Up Networking blog www.joinedupnetworking.com

Winning business – the secrets of developing great rapport
www.winningbusiness.net/downloads/pdfs/Rapport.pdf

ThinkFeelKnow www.thinkfeelknow.com

Think Feel Know is an international coaching and training company operating in the UK, USA and Australia, dedicated to the understanding and development of people. The Think Feel Know Model and Indicator are protected by Copyright © 2010 Think Feel Know Ltd. All Rights Reserved. Think Feel Know Limited is a company registered in the British Virgin Islands, registered number 1430938. For further information on Think Feel Know and how to apply it personally or within a business environment please visit www.thinkfeelknow.com

10

How to work a room

What topics are covered in this chapter?

- How to overcome nerves when meeting new people
- How to find the right people to talk to at a networking event
- How to circulate effortlessly and break into and out of conversations
- What to take with you when networking
- How to maximise your effectiveness when having a one-to-one meeting
- The etiquette of exchanging business cards

In the last chapter we showed you how to strike up a meaningful conversation with anyone you meet. In this chapter we will show you how to effortlessly find the right people to talk to in a room, so you can have that meaningful conversation.

There is a skill to working the room; however, this skill can be learned. You may be interested to know that a study of social fears undertaken in the USA identified that 'meeting new people in an unfamiliar environment' is nearly as stressful as unrehearsed public speaking.[1]

Overcoming nerves

> 'When meeting a stranger, and worrying whether you will be able to keep the conversation going, remember SW3 – Some Will, Some Won't, So What!'
>
> *Girish Shah, senior finance manager*

[1] www.ncbi.nlm.nih.gov/pmc/articles/PMC2262178/?tool=pubmed

Not everyone enjoys meeting new people. In fact, many professionals avoid attending networking events because of their dread and fears about meeting new people. Very often people are scared of rejection, or not knowing what to say. For example:

'What if I don't know what to say?'
'What if I get stuck in a conversation with someone very boring?'
'What happens if I can't find anyone to talk to?'

Most of these fears are not grounded in reality and are 'self-limiting beliefs' – i.e. things your subconscious tells you to protect you, but which limit your potential. There are many ways to overcome these nerves, for example:

■ Visualise, before an event, yourself having an enjoyable and fun time meeting new people.

■ Arrange to meet a friend or colleague at the event – but agree to split up and circulate.

■ Commit to attend a networking event regularly, as the more experience you have of working the room, the easier it becomes.

■ Practise your 'working the room' skills at big 'safe' social events.

■ Surf the news sites on the internet and find some topics which you would find interesting to discuss with people you meet, such as *'What do you think of the government's planned changes to …?'*

■ Remember that everyone who goes out networking is in the same position as you – they want to meet new people and have interesting conversations.

Finding the right people to talk to

The rules of a business gathering are different from a social gathering. People expect to meet people and circulate, and wouldn't be offended if you don't want to stay by their side all through the event. In fact, the very opposite is true – they may get very frustrated if you cling to them like a limpet all through the event.

> **"People expect to meet people and circulate"**

If you position yourself so that you can see people entering the room, you will be able to quickly spot friends, contacts, clients – even people you want to avoid! But here is the twist: you will be able to see people without seemingly breaking rapport or focus on the person you are talking to. There is nothing more off-putting than someone twisting their head to look around the room when they are talking to you.

If you have come specifically to meet a person, the best way to make sure this happens is to contact them before the event and arrange a time and place to meet, such as over lunch or during the first seminar session. Failing that, ask your event's host to introduce you to the person you want to meet.

At most business gatherings there is normally a formal part of the proceedings, be it a seminar, speaker or meal. As a busy professional you want to make the most out of the relationship-building opportunities when you sit down to this part of the proceedings.

Five minutes before the sit-down part of an event starts, ask your host to introduce you to one of the people you have come to the event to meet. After speaking to them for a few minutes, you then simply say, 'I'm enjoying our conversation, may I join you for the ...?'

If you've made the right impression, the answer will normally be 'yes' and you now have a huge opportunity to build upon your initial conversation and develop a deeper relationship during the formal event proceedings.

Why you need to circulate

As a busy professional you need to get the most out of your networking time. While networking should be fun and enjoyable, you need to be focused on what you planned to achieve at the event. This means you need to be evaluating the usefulness of each conversation you are having.

You may be having a very enjoyable conversation comparing notes on your new shoes with someone you have just met, but if they are unlikely in the short or medium term to help you meet your goals, then this becomes just a cosy conversation. The more time you spend having cosy conversations or speaking to random people not on your list, the less time you will have available to speak to the people you have come here to meet. Everyone at a networking event has come with the purpose of meeting people. So, no one will be offended if you don't talk to them for the whole evening. While there is nothing wrong with having only one or two really positive and engaging conversations at an event, you have missed out on the opportunity to speak to a whole room full of potential A-listers.

Normally about 5–10 minutes into a conversation you will know whether this is a useful connection or just a pleasant chat. At this point you need to make a decision before you break off the conversation and re-circulate: is this person an A-lister or a B-lister and therefore worth asking to meet up for a one-to-one in the future? If you think this person has the potential to become an A-lister for you, then spend a little longer getting to know them before asking to meet up for a one-to-one.

> **Tip**
>
> Maybe you've gone networking with someone else for moral support, but you will achieve more if you break up and tackle the room individually. You can then come back together at certain points and swap information and contacts which you have made.

I regularly attend face-to-face networking events and continue to be amazed by the number of people from the same company standing talking to each other. Why waste valuable networking time when they could have had that conversation in the office?

By dividing and conquering, a team of you can network with everyone in the room rather than just talking to the one or two brave souls who come up and talk with the gaggle of you in the corner.

Exiting from a conversation

There is a technique to exiting gracefully from a conversation. The golden rule is to never leave someone on their own. The best way to do this, and build up your social capital at the same time, is to introduce them to someone else and then make your excuses to leave. If no one comes to rescue you, there is nothing stopping you going to find another person to introduce to them – for example, in the queue for the drinks or the buffet. Or you could ask them who they would like to meet at the event and then aim to connect them.

Always aim to give a plausible reason to exit, for example nature calls or I've agreed to meet with a friend over lunch.

To exit yourself from a conversation, have a 'conversation ender' prepared. For example:

'I've really enjoyed talking to you, and I'm pleased to have met you. I'm guessing we have both come here to mix and meet people, and I don't want to monopolise you and stop you from meeting other people. Is there anyone here you want to meet? Perhaps I, or one of our hosts, can make the introduction for you?'

Breaking into a group

❝There is an art form to breaking into groups and conversations❞

Everyone at a networking event is looking to meet people. So logically, most people will be very welcoming if you come up and ask to speak to them. However, there is an art form to breaking into groups and conversations.

A room full of people is never static – conversations are always starting and ending, and people re-circulating. The way to spot whether a conversation is private or public is to look at how the group is standing. Any group which has an open side and people looking out to the group is likely to be happy to be joined by more people (see Figure 10.1). Any group where all the members are looking into the group and are 'effectively' closed is probably having a private conversation and doesn't want to be disturbed (Figure 10.2).

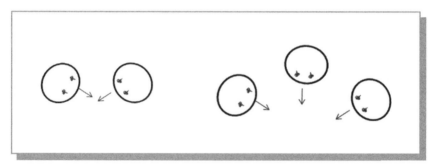

figure 10.1   An open pair and group

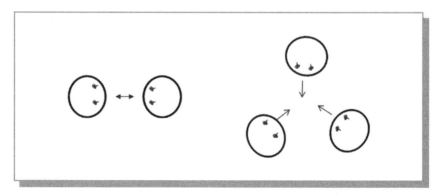

figure 10.2   A closed pair and group

When looking for a new group of people to join always look for someone standing on their own, or an open pair or group.

Don't just assume that a group of people will want you to join their conversation. As you approach the group, make eye contact and smile. Then ask the group,

'Is it OK if I join up?'

If the answer is 'no', don't take the rejection personally – their conversation was probably a private one.

However, there are times when you want to speak to someone in a closed group. A great tactic is to position yourself so you can see the group and wait until it changes formation, from closed to open. This is a sign that the conversation is losing its intensity and members of the group want to re-circulate, and it is appropriate for you to ask to join in the conversation. If the group shows no sign of changing formation, then hover around near the group and make eye contact with a member of the group – they are likely to ask you to join them.

> ### Tip
>
> Bring the quieter members of the group into the conversation. It will increase your social capital with them, but also give them an opportunity to contribute if they were struggling to get a word in.

As a last resort, if there is someone in the closed group you really want to speak to, approach the group, apologise for interrupting them and say you will only take up 30 seconds of their time. State that you would like to speak to Mr 'X' after they have finished their conversation, perhaps over lunch, and then depart from the group.

Changing a group's dynamic

If you find yourself in a closed group and want to change the dynamics of the conversation, position your body so that you are looking out of the group and make eye contact with people who are circulating near the group. This will encourage other people to join your group and naturally change the dynamic of the conversation.

Business card etiquette

When you hand over your business card, you are giving permission to be contacted by the other person. (You are not giving permission to go on to their mailing list!) Some people when networking literally go business card hunting and gathering. There is no benefit to coming back from an event with more than 100 business cards if you haven't taken the time to build a relationship with the other person. All this does is help increase a printer's business.

If you have enjoyed meeting someone and want to stay in touch with them, then ask them for their business card. For example:

'I've enjoyed talking to you today and would like to stay in touch with you. Can we swap business cards?'

Most people when asked for their business card will naturally provide it and ask for yours in return. Don't make the mistake of asking for someone's business card at the start of the conversation, as this gives the impression that you are just wanting to grab their contact details for a mailing list.

After you have met someone, use their business card to jot down some notes about them. Before you write on someone's business card, check that it is acceptable to do so. In some cultures, for example China, it is considered rude to write on someone else's business card.

Tip

Write down on a person's business card if they are happy to be signed up to your mailing list and connect with you on LindedIn and/or Twitter.

❝The notes that you make at the time of meeting may be invaluable❞

After a networking event, where you may have met up to 30 people, it's very hard to recall every single person or conversation that you had a week later. The notes that you make at the time of meeting may be invaluable for personalising future communications with them. Some ideas for what you can write down about them:

■ What they were wearing (if particularly memorable).

■ Personal details about them – children? hobbies? mutual connections?

■ Details about their company.

The contents of your networker's toolkit

Every networker should carry the following items:

■ Multiple copies of their business card.

■ Good quality biro and small notepad.

■ Name badge.

Your business card

A business card is still business's preferred way of exchanging contact details when meeting someone face-to-face. I suspect in the next ten years that physical business cards may be phased out in favour of virtual business cards, but until then we are stuck with actual physical business cards. Most companies will provide their client-facing employees with a business card. If you don't have your own card, or want a business card which is not branded with your employer's contact details, then get your own made up.

> **Tip**
>
> Print on both sides of your business card, but leave some white space for people to write on your card.

> **Tip**
>
> Don't choose a glossy or laminate finish for your business card. They may look impressive but are very hard for people to write on.

What needs to go on your business card (see Figure 10.3)?

■ Your name.

■ Your company name (if appropriate).

■ Your job title (if appropriate).

■ A mailing address – normally you now only need to include your email address rather than your physical address.

■ Phone numbers, preferably a direct line where you can always be reached.

■ Your company logo.

■ A tagline or description of the business – this can go on the back of
your card.

■ List of services or products – this can also go on the back of your card.

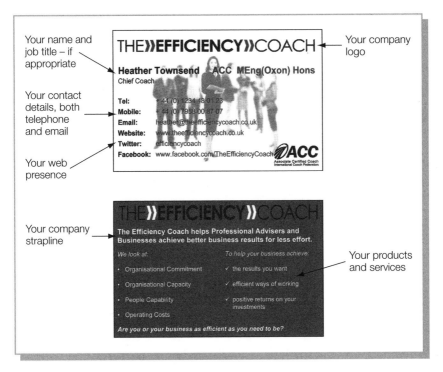

figure 10.3   **Details for your business card**

Good quality biro and small notepad

You may be thinking, why a biro? Many people's business cards are lami-
nated, and anything written using a wet ink, such as in a fountain pen,
easily rubs off on your hand … other business cards … your shirt pocket
… the inside of your handbag.

Make sure that you use a high-quality biro. A chewed-up, 'been-around-
the-block' biro is not going to leave people with the professional image
you have been trying to carefully craft. There is also nothing worse than
greeting people with ink-stained hands!

There are many ways that you can capture information for what you have
agreed to do for a new contact – for example on their business card, or on

your mini networking notepad. This notepad needs to be the size of a cigarette packet and easily fit into your handbag or your suit pocket.

Writing down what you've committed to do with your new contact shows that you are serious about developing a good quality relationship with your new contact. Most people will be very happy for you to say, 'If you don't mind, I'll just write that down so I don't forget'. Then, grab your notepad and quickly capture what you have just agreed to do.

Name badge

❝Make sure your name is in large lettering that people can read❞

A personalised name badge looks professional and makes sure that you always have a correctly spelled name badge regardless of how well organised the event is. Make sure your name is in large lettering that people can read without needing to reach for their glasses.

> **Tip**
>
> Choose a badge with a magnetic fastening, as these badges can be used on any outfit without damaging the fabric.

Making the most out of your one-to-one meetings

Many people you meet when networking will suggest that the two of you get together for a longer conversation – often called in networking circles 'a one-to-one'. If you are not sure whether you would benefit from a face-to-face meeting, then arrange a phone conversation first to 'get to know them better'.

> **Tip**
>
> If you have a lot of people you want to have a meeting with, then block out a day in your diary. Locate yourself in a hotel's lounge and arrange as many of these meetings for that day in the hotel lounge.

The aim of any one-to-one meeting is to strengthen the relationship. However, many people will have an agenda for this meeting. It may be to sell you something, or they are interested in buying your services. Early into a one-to-one meeting, remember to ask the other person:

'What are you looking to achieve in this meeting?'

If the conversation has gone well, towards the end of the meeting, ask:

'How can we help each other?' and *'Who do you know who would benefit from my services?'*

Summary

The skills needed for working a room can be learned, and may need to be practised if you are a shy person.

If you are targeting a specific person, contact them beforehand and arrange to meet them at the event.

Once you realise that a conversation is unproductive for you, work out a way to break off without offending the other person. If you meet an A-lister, then ask for a further one-to-one conversation.

Look to join open groups of people or individuals on their own.

If you want to stay in touch with someone, ask for their business card and suggest that you contact them in the coming weeks.

ACTION POINTS

■ When you are next looking for someone to talk to at a business or social gathering, have a go at making eye contact and smiling at someone you would like to speak to.

■ At your next face-to-face networking event, look for pairs and open groups to break into conversation with.

■ When standing talking with people, aim to keep the circle closed for the first five minutes so you can focus on the other person. Then open up a gap to allow others to join you.

■ When talking with people in a group, check to see whether everyone is interested and contributing to the conversation. Invite the quieter members of the group to contribute to the discussion.

■ If you don't have a business card, get one made up with your contact details on.

■ Next time you attend a face-to-face networking event, arrange to meet someone at the event.

■ If you go networking with a colleague, agree to split up and each work a different side of the room. At the end of the event compare notes.

■ Get an attendance list in advance of the event you are attending and divide up targets between all the people attending the event from your company. Agree in advance with the people attending from your company when you will reconvene and share information.

■ Have a go at attending a networking event on your own.

■ Next time you are out networking, write some details about each person you meet on their business card. Remember to capture these details on your client relationship management system.

Further resources

Books

Confident Networking for Career Success and Satisfaction, Gael Lindenfield and Stuart Lindenfield, Piatkus Books, 2005.

Networking Like A Pro: Turning contacts into connections, Ivan R. Misner, David C. Alexander and Brian Hilliard, Entrepreneur Press, 2010.

Brilliant Networking: What the best networkers, know, do and say, 2nd edition, Stephen D'Souza, Prentice Hall, 2010.

Nice Girls Don't Get the Corner Office, Lois Frankel, Little, Brown & Company, 2004.

Blogs and websites

Joined Up Networking www.joinedupnetworking.com

Winning business – the secrets of working a room www.winningbusiness.net/downloads/pdfs/WorkingRoom.pdf

11

How to build your own community

What topics are covered in this chapter?

- The personal benefits of building your own community
- The seven steps needed to create a successful and active community

In the last four chapters we have explored the skills professionals need to develop successful relationships through online and offline networking. In this chapter we will explore both 'why' you should consider developing a community from your network and 'how' to do this.

What is a community?

An active community is one where people meet and interact. Before social media burst on to the scene, this used to be limited to groups which met face-to-face, united by a common goal, interest or purpose. For example, a local residents' association, a football supporters' club, an amateur dramatics society or a professional association.

Online communities, such as a LinkedIn group, Facebook Fan or Business Page, are still built around common interests, but the exchange of ideas can happen 24 hours per day, and may extend across geographic borders.

Examples of communities I have created or joined:

■ My large Twitter following (5500 at time of writing).

■ A private virtual mastermind group, run by Paul Simister (www.plancs.co.uk), set up to help professionals help each other develop an income out of their product knowledge.

■ A private group of 20 bloggers committed to helping each other build valuable content and engaged readers for our blogs.

■ The Executive Village (www.executivevillage.co.uk), a virtual and face-to-face community of more than 400 business owners across the UK.

Why build your own community?

Having your own community puts you at the centre of your network. Imagine what it would be like if you could bring all your A-listers together in one place. And one place where you are seen to be at the centre of all worthwhile conversations.

When you have your own community, you become the main conduit or concierge to this community. Some professions, such as accountants and business coaches, naturally become concierges to their networks of clients. Think how powerful it would be to create a community out of this network – and how much value you could add back to your clients by introducing them all to each other.

As a concierge to your community, you can attract additional opportunities. For example, Sharon Gaskin (founder of The Trainers Training Company)[1] has built a community of 1200 trainers via LinkedIn. Her aim is to help trainers grow successful businesses, so she focuses her networking efforts on meeting freelance or newly freelancing trainers. Sharon benefits in three ways from her LinkedIn community. First, she enjoys having active contact with 1200 passionate trainers. Second, she is the hub, so she has a position which oversees everything that is happening. But most importantly, she is the focal point through which opportunities flow to the entire group.

Why do people join a community?

Humans have a need to belong and connect with others. People will join a community because they have had an experience, want to find some answers, meet like-minded people or want to be identified with a certain

---

[1] www.thetrainerstrainingcompany.co.uk

❝Humans have a need to belong and connect with others❞

community. For example, I became active with the local branch of the Chartered Institute of Personnel and Development because it enhanced my credibility as a learning and development specialist, but also increased my profile with potential local buyers of my services.

While people enjoy the feeling of belonging to a community, not everyone has the desire to contribute content or time to a community. Very often only a few community members will want to be actively involved in the discussions or the running of an event. Josh Bernoff and Charlene Li in their book *Groundswell*, identified the 90-9-1 rule for online communities: 1 per cent of your population will create content, 9 per cent will comment or engage with it, and 90 per cent will just browse or 'lurk'.[2]

Why people don't join or participate in an online community

There are many reasons why online communities are full of lurkers. First, there are millions of social networking sites available; most people don't have the time or inclination to contribute to every site. Some social networking sites can be very cliquey and often the online equivalent of entering a pub and feeling as if everyone has turned around and wondered why you have come in.

Steps to build your own community

1 What's the purpose of your community?

Beginning with your personal goals, decide on why you want to build your own community and what benefits it will bring the potential members. Starting a community because you want to keep close to your network is maybe a good reason, but not a powerful enough reason to attract members. What's in it for the people who join your community?

Be aware that what the community wants and actually does will evolve over time, which in the long term may not help you achieve your personal goals.

---

[2] Bernoff, J. and Li, C., *Groundswell*, Harvard Business School Press, 2008.

'There has to be a shared interest or topic which will bring people to your community – your sparkling personality is not enough.'

Mariam Cook, digital engagement expert[3]

2 Identify and find your members

Who is your ideal community member? Is it a potential client or perhaps existing clients, or both? Will you keep the membership of your community closed and by exclusive invitation only? Or will you let it be open to all?

---

case study The Executive Village[4]

The Executive Village has more than 400 business owners and senior decision makers, all of whom have to be approved before they can join. This community is a magnet for consultants and coaches. To keep the community balanced and not swamped with consultants, there are strict rules on the number of consultants, mentors and coaches who can join. In addition, anyone who isn't a senior decision maker within a business is denied membership of the group. This exclusivity actually makes the community more desirable to join!

You will need to be proactive to find the right members for your community. Unless you have celebrity status, don't expect that people will magically join as soon as you switch the group on. Having the right kind of early members, e.g. proactive advocates, in your community is vital for the success of your future community. Your early members need to be in the 10 per cent of people who will create content and comment on content. Remember the principle of social proof – people will want to join and actively participate if people like them are already present and contributing.

When you invite your first few members, include in the invitation how they will personally benefit from joining the community – and how they can personally help grow a vibrant community.

3 Create visible guidelines for your community

Unless you educate your community about what is acceptable behaviour and what isn't you risk building an online community with poor-quality

---

[3] http://uk.linkedin.com/pub/mariam-cook/5/224/a8a
[4] www.theefficiencycoach.co.uk/executivevillage.php

content and low-value conversations. For example, will you allow people to post content which blatantly advertises their services? Will you specify criteria which potential members need to satisfy before they can join? Many companies aim to stay in contact with their alumni, for instance. Unsurprisingly, entry to these companies' alumni communities is dependent on whether you have worked for them.

Make sure you prominently display these guidelines and stick to them. I can promise you that you will have to deal with people transgressing the rules of your community. Sadly, I regularly have to purge my Facebook groups and Twitter followers of spammers who want to entice me to click through to a porn site. But not everyone is a clear-cut spammer. For example, what about the recruiter, even though it is against the rules of your community, who occasionally posts about a job vacancy? Or the blogger who posts up a blog which is a thinly veiled advert for their products? Or the member in your networking group who keeps on selling to people? Have you thought about how you are going to moderate your community and manage unacceptable behaviour? One strike and you are out, or a friendly warning first?

> **❝Not everyone is a clear-cut spammer❞**

4 Where will you host your community?

'Unless you have enough spare time and resource to build a social website from scratch, first think about using a 'plug in and go' solution to host your community.'

Mariam Cook, digital engagement expert

Your members will need a place to meet – whether face-to-face or online. For your online network, will you use a groups feature on a big social networking site, such as LinkedIn's Groups[5] feature or a Yahoo Group, or set up your own Facebook community or business page?[6] Or is the right 'venue' your own fully customisable social network, such as Ning,[7] Buddypress[8] or SocialGO?[9]

---

[5] www.linkedin.com/directory/groups
[6] www.facebook.com/pages/create.php?
[7] www.ning.com
[8] www.buddypress.org
[9] www.socialgo.com

5 Fine-tune and seed content before going public

A community is a living organism. Unless it has died, it is never static, and the dynamics of the community will change over time. Personally invite your first handful of members and ask them to seed content and proactively comment on posts and discussions. Once you have some content within your site, consider making the community public. No one likes joining the online equivalent of a ghost town.

6 Maintaining momentum

An active group, regardless of whether it meets face-to-face or online, which has a genuine sense of community, will attract more like-minded individuals. The principle of social proof tells us that people like to be identified with successful communities. This means that your aim as the founder of the community is to get to the point where members invite their friends and network to join because it is a great place to hang out.

To create the environment where your members invite others to join, think about regularly doing the following:

■ Spend time encouraging and rewarding contribution. How can you generate status for members of your community who contribute to the success of the community?

■ Include an area within the online forum or a mechanism for face-to-face groups where new members can introduce themselves and start to engage with the group.

■ Make it easy for people to join the conversation, such as asking questions which invite a response.

■ Ask for feedback from the community on how the community could be improved for the members.

■ Run face-to-face or online events for the community.

■ Welcome criticism and healthy debate – but respond positively to any negative comments.

■ Have regular communications to the members of the community, e.g. newsletters or broadcasts.

As the community grows it becomes harder to run and moderate it by yourself. Create a management team with defined roles and responsibilities within the community to spread the load. This management team could be regional champions, moderators or the more traditional face-to-face community leadership structure, e.g. chairperson, treasurer, membership advisor, secretary, fundraiser/events organiser.

7 Promote your community

❝Where do potential members of your community hang out?❞

Unless you want your community to be one of the best-kept secrets, you will still need to promote it. How can you automate the process of finding new members for the community? Where can you talk about it? Where do potential members of your community hang out?

Different ways in which you can promote your community include:

- on your business card
- advertise on your email signature
- write about your community on your newsletters and mail shots
- on your LinkedIn or Facebook status updates
- within other communities of which you are a member
- tweet about the community.

Summary

Building your own community takes a lot of effort on your part, but the reward is professional credibility.

The seven steps to building and maintaining a community:

1 Decide on the purpose of the community.

2 Identify and find your members.

3 Create guidelines for membership.

4 Decide where you will meet.

5 Fine-tune and seed content before you publicly launch your community.

6 Maintain momentum and interaction.

7 Promote your community.

ACTION POINTS

■ What do your A-listers like to talk about and discuss? How could you set up an online community to meet that need? What would be your membership criteria and rules of the group?

■ What clubs or societies would your A-listers already belong to and you would enjoy being a member of? How could you play an active part within the club?

■ How could you build a community with influential people within your company?

■ Volunteer to be a moderator for one of the online communities in which you regularly participate.

■ If you already run an online community, think of three ways in which you can encourage more participation within your community.

■ What group, such as a mastermind group, could you set up to strengthen your networking with your A-listers?

Further resources

Books

Managing Online Forums, Patrick O'Keefe, Amacom, 2008.

Groundswell, Josh Bernoff and Charlene Li, Harvard Business School Press, 2008.

The Tipping Point, Malcolm Gladwell, Abacus, 2001.

Online community hosting

Yahoo groups http://uk.groups.yahoo.com

LinkedIn groups www.linkedin.com/directory/groups

Facebook groups www.facebook.com/groups

Facebook business and community pages www.facebook.com/pages/create.php?

Ning www.ning.com

Buddypress www.buddypress.org

SocialGO www.socialgo.com

12

Networking across cultural barriers

What topics are covered in this chapter?

- How to use online networking to break down cultural differences
- How to fit in and relate to people, regardless of the cultural, geographical and social differences between you
- When it is appropriate and expected to show emotion
- What is the appropriate greeting for a stranger in different cultures
- How to adapt your language when talking with non-native speakers
- How to change your discussion style, depending on the culture you are in
- When and how to exchange business cards

'As global virtual teams become increasingly prevalent, a successful professional has to find ways to work across organisational, cultural, functional and geographical boundaries.'

Hamish Taylor, Shinergise Partners Ltd

The media has incorrectly been telling us for many years that the world is getting smaller. It's actually the rapid advancement in communications technology which has made the world feel smaller. Twenty-five years ago letters which took weeks to arrive were the norm for international communications as expensive international phone calls were saved for special occasions – and email was very much in its infancy. Fast forward to today, and many people don't think twice about sending an email across to the other side of the world, or making a free or cheap international video call to foreign climes. Email and the internet have enabled international communication to happen simply, rapidly and cheaply. Even though international communication is now as easy as making a local phone call, cultural differences persist – and will persist for the foreseeable future. Today's networker, to succeed in the global marketplace, now more than ever, has to be aware of the cultural differences that exist. In this chapter we will look at the skills and awareness that a networker needs to successfully build relationships regardless of what international culture they are working in or across.

Online networking as an enabler

'We look at how they dress, we look at the houses that they live in, and the cars they drive and then we label people.'

Sharon Carville, the HR dept

Our brains are programmed to make assumptions based on material possessions, appearances and how a person speaks. They do this because historically our very survival rested on how quickly we made a judgement on whether they were friend or foe. As we found out in Chapter 10, the more shared common interests, the more likely rapport

❝Online communication tends to be solely by the written word❞

and a relationship will develop between two people. Online communication tends to be solely by the written word. This means that cultural differences which are often emphasised by appearances, material possessions, body language and verbal language are very often not apparent. This means we may also miss the visual and audible clues which might cause us to approach a person in a different manner. This means it is worth spending longer building up a relationship online before moving to a face-to-face or telephone meeting.

Observe and adapt

'There are more differences between people than there are between cultures. These are mostly behavioural style differences rather than necessarily cultural differences.'

Ivan Misner, founder of BNI

People within a distinct culture have different beliefs, attitudes and ways of doing things. Everyone is slightly different – no two people are actually

100 per cent alike in both mind and body. You see these microcosms of culture also happening within a business. Different teams, departments and offices within a single business will all have slightly different cultures, or more simply different 'ways of thinking and doing'. The organisation may be tightly bound together by commonly held values and beliefs, but not everyone will interpret or act on these in the same way. A floor with an open-plan office, within the same building, will have a different feel and vibe to a floor where some individuals have their own offices.

Successful networkers are aware of potential differences between people and behaviours – and are continually on the lookout for signs which give them clues about 'what are acceptable behaviours, and what are not'. Expertly networking across different cultures is more than just being able to rapidly adjust and conform to expected behaviour. Your research before travelling or meeting anyone from a different background to yourself will give you clues to watch out for and what to expect. For example, what is the appropriate greeting for a stranger and a friend? When is it OK to shake a woman's hand? How should you exchange business cards? What's the typical style for a discussion? Does a meeting timetabled for 15:00 really mean it will start at 15:00?

As the saying goes, when in Rome, do as the Romans do.

Expressive versus reserved cultures

There are lots of examples where we see cultural stereotypes being used, especially in comedy. The British are always portrayed as being reserved. Some of the southern European cultures are shown as being very loud and waving their arms around when they talk. Some Asian cultures are depicted as ultra-polite. While we have to be careful not to automatically label people we meet, it is helpful to at least be on the lookout for behaviours in business people which are different to our own. If you are talking with someone from an expressive culture, for example an Italian, you would expect more 'feel'-type communication, whereas with someone from a reserved culture, such as Japan, you would see more 'know' and 'think' types of communication. To increase your ability to relate and connect with someone from a different cultural background to you, listen out for the amount of 'feel'-type communication and adapt the amount of emotion and feeling you display to match their level.

The websites Executive Planet (www.executiveplanet.com), Kwintessential (www.kwintessential.co.uk/resources/country-profiles.html) and Cyborlink (www.cyborlink.com) have some guidelines which you should read prior to meeting with people from other countries.

Reserved	Expressive
UK	Southern Europe
Japan	Middle East
Northern Europe	Egypt
Ethiopia	Russia
China	South America

Unsurprisingly, the degree of expressiveness within a culture heavily influences people's preference for one of the three communication styles – think, feel or know.

Communication style	Preference
Think	UK, Japan
Feel	Southern Europe
Know	Scandinavia, Germany, Austria

Appropriate greetings

From the formal British handshake to the reserved Japanese bow to the French spontaneous kiss on both cheeks, greeting people – whether a stranger or a good friend – varies across different cultures. The more expressive a culture, the more likely the greeting will involve closeness of physical contact. The greeting of a kiss on both cheeks favoured by the expressive Mediterranean cultures requires both parties to fully enter each other's personal space, whereas a handshake, the preferred greeting used by the reserved British and Americans, requires far less invasion of each other's personal space.

> **Tip**
>
> If you are in a situation where you are wondering what an appropriate greeting is, follow the example given by others around you.

It is worth noting that some religions, for example Islam, forbid physical contact between unmarried or non-related men and women. As a rule of thumb, if a religion requires women to cover their face or hair, then there is a strong likelihood that a handshake – or any physical contact with a man who she is not related to – is deemed inappropriate behaviour.

Language and the spoken word

I find one of the most effective opening questions to be 'How's it going?' in whatever the local informal style of asking is, e.g. 'Do desu-ka?' is Japanese for 'How is it?'

Hamish Taylor, Shinergise Partners

English may be the predominant language used in international business, but a trip to America or even places in the UK with a strong regional dialect and accent, such as the North East, will demonstrate that the English language is used very differently in different geographical locations. When you are communicating with non-native English speakers, eliminate any slang or colloquialisms, as these may lead to misunderstandings. Something as simple as saying, 'Keep me in the loop' in Africa means to get a woman pregnant.

For example, instead of saying,

'Give me a bell' or *'Drop me a line'*, say:

'Let's arrange a time for a telephone call' or *'Please send me an email.'*

When someone is communicating in a language with which they are not fully familiar, they will have a tendency to say 'yes' to any question – even if they do not fully understand the question. Therefore, use open-ended questions or phrases which test their understanding, e.g.

'Please summarise your understanding for me.' rather than

'Can you tell me what you need to do?'

❝In Anglo-Saxon cultures, silence is seen to be uncomfortable❞ Different cultures have different styles of discussions. In Anglo-Saxon cultures, silence is seen to be uncomfortable, and someone will start talking when someone else finishes speaking. Interrupting someone before they have finished talking is seen to be rude. Yet the Latin temperaments will happily tolerate a small amount of interruption as this is seen to be a sign of interest in the subject, rather than rudeness. The Oriental cultures like to have time to reflect on and digest what has been said, as this shows respect for the person who has been talking. Therefore, when you are talking with an Oriental, expect silences in a discussion and any interruptions in conversation will be seen as disrespectful.

> **Tip**
>
> Whenever you are attempting to speak a little in a foreign language, always smile – as this will make you seem more welcoming and help break the ice.

When you need to engage cross-culturally, take the time to learn the basics of please, thank you, yes, no, good morning, etc. If you find that you are a regular visitor to a country where you are not a native speaker of the language, take the time to learn a little more of the language, for example 'No problem' in that language. When Hamish Taylor, partner at Shinergise, is running workshops in different countries, he finds that using a few words of the delegate's native language builds engagement and helps to create connectivity between people.

Business cards

Cultural etiquette often defines how a business card should be given, received and treated – and this will differ from country to country. Before you visit a foreign country, ask a local how business cards are used. For example, here is the business card etiquette for Japan.

If you travel to Japan and meet people, business cards are expected and a 'must carry'. To show respect for your Japanese hosts, use double-sided business cards, one side printed in your native language, the other in Japanese. When business cards are exchanged, always present your business card (with Japanese language side face up) to the most senior member of the Japanese party first. Similarly, when receiving a business card, take it in both hands and say 'Thank you' or the Japanese for 'Thank you' – 'Hajimemashite'. At the end of a meeting, remember to take all the business cards and put them in your business card holder. And finally, never write notes on or even play or fiddle with a Japanese business card.

Rules-based culture versus relationship-based culture

If you break the rules of rules-based cultures there are often heavy social and legal consequences – for example, jumping a queue in the UK or crossing the road without using the pedestrian crossing in the USA – whereas relationship-based cultures place more value on the relationship than the rule. The relationship must be preserved first, rather than adhering to the society's rules. Having knowledge of whether a culture has a tendency to put the rule before the relationship is important for a networker. To generate opportunities within a relationship-based culture means it is even more about 'who you know or are related to' rather than 'what you know'.

Rules-based cultures	Relationship-based cultures
North America	Southern Europe (France, Italy, Spain, etc.)
UK	South America
Northern Europe	Middle East
Australia	

If you are networking within a relationship-based culture, make sure you spend more time on developing the relationship before starting to talk business.

Punctuality and time

Some cultures like people to be organised and to stay focused on the job at hand; others are quite comfortable with people multi-tasking and being spontaneous. Let me illustrate with two examples.

1 In the UK, if you entered someone's office and they were talking on the phone, you would discreetly sit down, avoid eye contact, and the person would close off their phone call before greeting you. By contrast, last year I did exactly the same in Rome and the speaker stood up, walked around the desk, greeted me with hugs *and* continued his telephone conversation!

2 Still in Rome, I later attended a meeting which began fully 40 minutes late! Then, during the meeting, people were freely making mobile phone calls, completing forms which were totally unrelated to the meeting *and* they addressed issues which were on the meeting agenda. It seemed to my British eyes that the meeting was a mess; however, everyone was quite at ease and the meeting achieved all it needed to do.

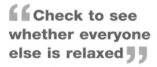
Check to see whether everyone else is relaxed

The moral is that when you see something which makes you uncomfortable, check to see whether everyone else is relaxed, and if they are, simply go with the flow.

In some cultures punctuality and order are very important. In these cultures, a host would be horrified if a guest turned up late or unannounced – would there be enough food for everyone? In fact, here in the UK, you are often given a window of time when you should turn up – how often do you see on an invite '18:30 for 19:00'? However, in cultures where punctuality and order are not as important, the host has probably made extra food just in case a few extra people turn up. In Mediterranean Europe times given can be approximately 15 minutes out, but in the Middle East and Africa a time given could mean any time that day.

Punctuality and order important	*Punctuality and order less important*
UK	South America
North America	Middle East
Asia	Africa
Australasia	Southern Europe

Relating to anyone you meet, regardless of where they are from

'Understand the differences; act on the commonalities.'

Andrew Masondo, African National Congress

A relationship is built upon shared values and trust. When you meet someone from a different economic, cultural or social background it is all too easy to see the differences. A business contact of mine, David Stoch,[1] is a very nice guy with this profile: he is young, male, single, from South Africa and lives alone in a suburb of London. By contrast, I am older, female, British, married, two kids and I live in the country. On the face of it we are very different and from very different backgrounds. On a casual lunch one day, we discovered a mutual interest in classical and jazz music, and this has become the common ground which bonds us together when working on projects.

When you meet someone different to you, use basic human shared values to connect with them. For example, pretty much everyone is proud of their family and home. A business owner will almost always be passionate about their business – and want to talk about it. BNI, the world's largest net-

---

[1] www.meerkatpr.co.uk

working organisation, has operations in 44 countries. Each time they have launched in a new country they have been told that BNI wouldn't work here because the culture is different. The success of BNI tells a different story. They have found that business owners everywhere in the world are keen to work together to help each other grow their business – regardless of the dominant culture in which they are operating.

Most people will have hobbies and interests outside of work. What do they like to watch or listen to? What do they do to relax? What type of sport do they like to watch, follow or take part in?

If you look for differences you will find them; if you look for the similarities you will also find them. This is why it is important when building a relationship with someone unfamiliar to you to look for the similarities and shared interests. Start by trusting the other person – trust their intentions and motivations, and open with a big happy smile – it will break all cultural barriers. You can always change your mind later.

Summary

When you are networking with people from different social, economic or cultural backgrounds, focus on areas of common interest and look for the similarities rather than the differences.

When networking in a place or country unfamiliar to yourself, research on the internet so that you know what to expect, and find a local guide or coach to help you fit in and understand appropriate behaviours and social etiquette.

To help engage and connect with people who do not speak your language, take the time to learn a few phrases of the local language.

Time is viewed differently by different cultures. In some cultures give yourself more time between meetings and appointments.

Watch and observe what the locals do when out meeting and greeting people. Follow their example and you probably won't go far wrong.

ACTION POINTS

■ Next time you visit a foreign country, buy a guide book and learn a few phrases of the native tongue.

■ For a week, try to spend an hour a day without using any jargon, slang or colloquialism when you talk.

■ If you regularly visit a country where the native tongue is not English, get the back of your business card translated into the country's native tongue.

■ Find an expat living in the UK and ask how different life and culture is in their home country.

■ Find someone at your work who is of a different social, economic or cultural background to you. Take the time to find out what you have in common, rather than looking for the differences. How easily does the relationship seem to form?

Further resources

Books

Kiss, Bow or Shake Hands, Terri Morrison and Wayne A. Conaway, Adams Media Corporation, 2006.

Riding the Waves of Culture: Understanding cultural diversity in business, Fons Trompenaars and Charles Hampden-Turner, Nicholas Brealey Publishing, 1997.

Websites and blogs

Executive Planet www.executiveplanet.com

Kwintessential www.kwintessetial.co.uk/resources/country-profiles.html

Cyborlink www.cyborlink.com

Putting your joined up approach to networking into action

So far in this book we have looked at the behaviours, attitudes and skills needed to be a successful networker. In the last part of the book we are going to put it all together and build a personal networking strategy and action plan for you, to help you achieve career and business success.

13

Building your own successful joined up networking strategy

What topics are covered in this chapter?

- How to build a successful joined up networking strategy
- How to build a network of people who help you achieve your business and career goals
- Where to meet great people for your network
- How to measure your effectiveness as a networker

So far in this book we have looked at the behaviours, attitudes and skills needed to be a successful networker. Now, we are going to put it all together and build a personal networking strategy and action plan for you, to help you achieve career and business success.

'98 per cent of people have generated business via word of mouth, only 3 per cent have a strategy to do so.'

BNI research

There are six key steps to building a successful joined up networking strategy and plan. A joined up networking strategy is one where you are using both face-to-face and online networking tools and techniques:

- Set goals and objectives.
- Identify who you need in your network.
- Analyse the state of your current network.

■ Decide where you will meet the right people for your network.

■ Decide how to measure your effectiveness as a networker.

■ Write out your networking action plan (this step will be covered in the next chapter).

Setting your networking goals

'The number one reason why some people get work done faster is because they are absolutely clear about their goals and objectives and don't deviate from them.'

Brian Tracy, author of Eat That Frog![1]

❛❛Your personal networking journey may take you outside of your comfort zone❜❜ Take a moment to reflect on why you picked up this book and decided to read it. What was it particularly about business networking, your business or your career which compelled you to read a book on the subject? There has to be some personal motivation on your part to understand more about networking – most people don't get up in the morning and decide, 'I know, I will read a book on business networking'. Your personal networking journey may take you outside of your comfort zone and possibly force you to confront some of your personal fears. At these points in time, knowing why you are doing what you are doing, and the prize waiting at the end of it, will often mean the difference between success and failure.

So, let's explore your motivation to improve your knowledge and skills about business networking.

■ What are you hoping to achieve more of, for less time and effort, by improving your ability to network?

■ If I could wave a magic wand and grant you one wish, what would you ask for? More business, a promotion, a better job, a bigger support network?

'Only about 3 per cent of adults have clear written goals. These people accomplish five and ten times as much as people of equal or better education and ability but have, for whatever reason, taken the time to write out exactly what it is they want.'

Brian Tracy, author of Eat That Frog!

[1] Tracy, B., *Eat that Frog! Get more of the important things done – today!* Berrett-Koehler Publishers, Inc, 2002.

Close your eyes for a few moments and try to visualise what success you want to achieve. What does your inner voice say to you? What do you see in your mind's eye? What feelings are you experiencing?

Then, complete this sentence:

My networking strategy will help me achieve _____ (*fill in with what it will help you achieve*) by _____ (*fill in with a date by when you want to achieve this*).

Here are some examples of networking goals:

My networking strategy will help me find a new job of equal or better pay, less than an hour's travel from my house, working for a retailing company, by Dec 31st.

My networking strategy will help me find five new clients every month, each one spending at least £500 with me, by Dec 31st.

My networking strategy will help me fill the current vacancies within the finance team, without having to use a recruitment agency, by Dec 31st.

My networking strategy will help me to find a publisher to commission my book, by Dec 31st.

Now take a look at what you have just written and be honest with yourself.

1 Is this your goal? You are far more likely to achieve your personal goal if you make your goal your own, rather than trying to achieve someone else's goals for you.

2 Is this goal realistic? For example, growing your business by ten times in the space of three months by networking alone is probably not realistic.

3 Does your goal have a fixed date? Summer is not a fixed date, 31st July is a fixed date.

4 Can you measure your goal to know whether you have succeeded or failed? 'Be a better networker' is not a measurable specific goal. 'Win five new clients for the next three months' is measurable *and* specific

5 Is your goal *specific*? Can your goal be visualised? For example, you can easily visualise a monthly report showing five new clients being won each month.

If you have answered 'no' to any of these five questions, then go back and revisit your networking goal(s) until you have them right.

Identifying who you need in your network

In Chapter 7 we coined the phrase 'A-lister' to define the person who is most likely to be able to help you achieve your goals. However, we will begin by profiling your ideal client, since this is the key to choosing the most appropriate A-lister.

> **Tip**
>
> If you are reading this chapter and thinking 'but I want my network to help me accelerate my career, not generate business', you are still involved in selling something. It just so happens that the product or service you are selling is you, and your ideal client is a new boss or new employer.

Thinking about your ideal client, how much do you know about their:

- industry sector
- position or job title
- reading preferences
- social networking site memberships
- hobbies or interests outside of work
- habits, behaviours, personality types?

Connectors

In his book *The Tipping Point*, Malcolm Gladwell identified a special type of networker called a 'connector'.[2] These are people who are able to naturally maintain a high level of influence within a network of people significantly bigger than that of the average person. Their large networks span many different professions, social and cultural circles. But more importantly for networkers, connectors make a habit of regularly introducing people within their networks. Gladwell discovered that true connectors are quite rare – they number about one person in several thousand.

While a connector may not, on first sight, be naturally an A-lister for you, the sheer size and influence they wield within their network means they have the potential to regularly introduce you to the people you do want to meet.

---

[2] Gladwell, M., *The Tipping Point*, Abacus, 2001.

Gatekeepers

Your A-listers are very likely to be people who are 'gatekeepers' to a network which contains a high percentage of your ideal client. Gatekeepers already have a large and well-established network, and are seen to be at the 'hub' of this network. To make your networking as efficient as possible, your aim needs to be to find and generate strong relationships with as many gatekeepers to your ideal client as possible. For example, Sharon Gaskin, managing director of The Trainers Training Company,[3] is a gatekeeper to a network of more than 1000 self-employed trainers.

❝Your aim needs to be to find and generate strong relationships❞

If you identify an A-lister who is a gatekeeper, you need to develop a strong relationship with them, so that you increase the probability of receiving referrals. This is why it pays to focus your networking time and attention on A-listers who happen to be gatekeepers.

To help you think about where to look for gatekeepers, fill in a client analysis worksheet for each of your ideal clients, and who may be well connected to them, based on their personal preferences. (This worksheet is available to download at www.joinedupnetworking.com.)

Take a look at your client analysis worksheet to help you identify who should be in your network:

■ Who is well connected to my target client?

■ Who do I know who is a gatekeeper to a large network of my target client?

■ Do I know any connectors?

When you are networking, you need to be on the lookout for ideal clients, new A-listers, connectors and gatekeepers.

Analysing the state of your network

There are three main activities in the growth of a productive network:

■ Building connections.

■ Deepening existing relationships.

■ Pruning connections.

---

[3] www.thetrainerstrainingcompany.co.uk

	Ideal client	Where will they 'hang out'?	Who else will be connected to them?
Industry sector	Accountant	ICAEW events	Lawyers
		Chambers of Commerce events	IFAs
		4N and BNI	
		Professional seminars	
Level in their organisation			
Age	30–60		
Reading preferences		Accountancy Age	
Social networking site memberships	Accounting Web		
	Twitter		
	UK Business Forums		
Hobbies or interests outside of work		Potential school governor?	
		Scouts	
		Sporting club member	
Habits, behaviours, personality types	Introverted, likes numbers		
Family status		School events	Parents at the school

A successful networker will be doing all three activities simultaneously. However, there will be times when there will need to be more focus on one of the three activities. For example, when I had my first child I switched my networking focus so that I could build up a network of local first-time mums to support me through my transition to motherhood. After two years as a business owner, 70 per cent of my networking time and effort is now spent deepening existing relationships, rather than actively cultivating new connections.

As a busy professional you need to focus your networking efforts on the connections which give you the greatest rate of return – whether that is support, friendship, answers or new business. It is impossible to keep every relationship strong and current; inevitably some people in your network will naturally fall away. Very occasionally, you may need to reassess a relationship and prune it from your network; perhaps the relationship has gone sour, circumstances have changed or your credibility is being damaged by being close to this person. At its most severe, pruning may involve disconnecting yourself from a contact on a social network. Pruning your network may sound a drastic step, but it is very similar to the reasons why we prune a fruit tree – the act of pruning makes the fruit tree stronger and better prepared to yield a bigger crop next year.

Think about your personal network. Is it in a state to help you easily achieve your networking goals? What approximate percentage of time do you need to spend on building, deepening or pruning?

Analysing the state of your relationships

There are five different levels to a relationship

Level 1: 'identify'

At this level, you have just become aware of this contact. Maybe someone has mentioned them in a conversation; perhaps you have seen a tweet of them or seen their name on an attendance list at an event.

Level 2: 'engage'

At this point you have physically or virtually met a contact and started a conversation. For example, you may have talked to them at a face-to-face networking event, or exchanged some tweets or posts within an online forum. At this point in time you are very unlikely to recommend them or their services to others.

❝You have taken a conscious decision to strengthen the relationship❞

Level 3: 'strengthen'

At this stage of the relationship, you have taken a conscious decision to strengthen the relationship. This means that you have taken the time to have a one-to-one meeting with them, whether in person or by phone.

Level 4: 'collaborate'

The trust has built within the relationship to the point where you have agreed to help each other, pass referrals and potentially actively look for ways to work together.

Level 5: 'inner circle'

The relationship is now such that you have worked together and regularly recommend each other's services. There is a strong possibility that your relationship has moved from a purely professional relationship into a personal friendship.

Think about people in your network who you consider to be your A-listers or potential clients. Your relationship needs to be at least at Level 3. At what level is the state of your relationship with them? Who do you need to spend more time with to increase the level of trust and collaboration in the relationship?

---

case study   Mike Briercliffe

Mike is a natural connector, and is the hub of many different personal and professional networks. He uses various online networking tools to manage his contacts at the different stages of his relationship with them.

Level 1: 'identify'. Over the past two years Twitter has become Mike's main mechanism for identifying new potential members for his network.

Level 2: 'engage'. When Mike starts to have a conversation with a potential connection, he will strengthen the relationship by inviting them to connect with him on LinkedIn.

Level 3: 'strengthen'. At the point that the trust starts to build and Mike sees some potential in the relationship going further, he will take the relationship offline and suggest a phone call or one-to-one meeting.

Level 4: 'collaborate'. Mike will use both LinkedIn and Twitter to maintain a regular conversation with those people he trusts and will recommend.

Level 5: 'inner circle'. At this point, Mike has worked with this person, trusts them explicitly and they will have been invited to join his personal social network on Ning and black book of trusted contacts.

case study   Jay Blake

Jay runs Ichthus Video, a video production company which specialises in working with professional communicators such as marketing agencies. His business has been solely marketed through networking. Jay uses a mixture of face-to-face events, online networking tools as well as a CRM system to keep track of his conversations.

Level 1: 'identify'. Typically, Jay will identify new members of his network, through personal recommendation, Twitter or meeting them at a face-to-face networking event hosted by 4Networking or NRG.

Level 2: 'engage'. Jay uses the one-to-one time in a 4Networking meeting to engage with the people he has identified who he would like to meet in the room. With NRG, typically he will know who he would like to meet in advance and arrange to meet them at the meeting. Any conversations which Jay has in person will always be backed up with a request to connect on LinkedIn or Twitter to keep the conversations going.

Level 3: 'strengthen'. At this point, Jay requests an in-person meeting or a Skype™ call to deepen the relationship. One of the techniques which Jay uses to stay memorable – regardless of whether it is a virtual meeting or face-to-face meeting – is to provide homemade cake. As you can imagine, this is a great way to build his social capital with his network.

Level 4: 'collaborate'. Jay uses both online and offline networking methods to maintain communication with the people he trusts and recommends. As well as using Twitter and LinkedIn to stay in touch, he will deliberately choose to attend a networking event when he knows that any of his Level 4 or 5 type connections are attending.

Level 5: 'inner circle'. Jay calls his inner circle his 'one hundred club' and aims to have 100 A-listers within his inner circle. He tags any prospective A-listers in his customer relationship management system as a 'one hundred club' member. Every month he runs off a report from his CRM system to proactively talk to every member of his one hundred club every three months.

case study   Helen Stothard

Helen runs HLS Business Solutions, a virtual assistant business. Helen's team and clients are spread right across the UK and Europe. She has never advertised her business and has generated all her clients, suppliers and team members via her networking activities. Helen's sole aim when networking is to build strong relationships with advocates for her and her business.

Level 1: 'identify'. Helen initially meets potential members for her network from online forums, Twitter and a community of virtual assistants called VASG.

Level 2: 'engage'. Helen will start conversations on the online forums and Twitter. She builds up the relationships first by proactively sharing advice and knowledge.

Level 3: 'strengthen'. Normally, Helen's network will initiate a conversation with her – generally via Skype, but as many in her network are more than an hour's travel away, very rarely in person.

Level 4: 'collaborate'. When Helen has either started to work for, recommend or use a person in her network, she aims to find a way to meet in person – often when either her clients are holidaying near to her or she will deliberately plan a weekend away near to someone she wants to meet in person.

Level 5: 'inner circle'. For Helen's trusted contacts, she connects with them socially and uses Facebook to keep the relationship personal as well as professional.

Deciding where to network

'A successful networker will fish in a pond well stocked with big fishes.'

Jon Baker, venture-Now

Once you have identified who you want to meet and why you want to meet them, the next stage is to identify where you are going to meet them.

❝There is no right or wrong answer about where to network❞

If you need some ideas on where you can meet people, look back to Chapters 4 and 5 for all the different online and face-to-face networking available. There is no right or wrong answer about where to network – however, for your networking to be effective you need first to be clear on what you want to achieve from your networking.

> **Tip**
>
> To find an online forum for a certain type of person or interest, do a Google search for 'online forum xxx', e.g. online forum lawyers, online forum parents.

There is no easy way to find the best places to network. You need to be prepared to do your research and experiment with events and groups, as not every group, event or forum will work for everyone – see Table 13.1.

- Ask around and do some internet searches, i.e. where do your competitors and peers hang out?
- Attend a few networking groups as a guest.
- Attend some events hosted by your professional association.

> **Tip**
>
> To find local networking events and groups targeted at small businesses, do a Google search for 'business networking xxxx' or 'professional networking xxxx', e.g. business networking Bedford.

Table 13.1 Types of networking best suited to different networking goals

You want to:	Try:
Enhance your profile	Mix-and-mingle type events, Twitter, online forums, speaking at events, professional association events, write a blog
Generate new business	Referral generation clubs (particularly if you target small businesses), Twitter, blogging, conferences
Find answers and solutions	Mastermind groups, online forums, professional association events, reading blogs
Build your community	Voluntary, special interest or community groups, mastermind groups, online forums, social events
Find a new job	Social events, professional association events, LinkedIn, blogging

There is a plethora of online networking sites around (see Chapter 5). The vast range of online networking sites gives the networker the option of using different sites to categorise the state of their relationship with a person. For example, I will connect with most people on LinkedIn, and follow most genuine people back on Twitter, but I will only connect with people on my personal Facebook account if I would be happy to invite them to my house for dinner.

<hr>

case study   Bryony Thomas

Bryony has developed a joined up networking strategy which has allowed her to successfully source locally based clients for her marketing consultancy, Clear Thought. The aim of her networking strategy is to develop a strong locally based network of clients, referrers and suppliers. She has achieved great results by ruthlessly and consistently applying her joined up networking strategy over the past two years. This rigour and discipline have allowed her to build a business which has billed over £400,000 through its network of marketing suppliers in its first two years of business.

She uses Twitter to complement her locally based face-to-face networking. When she is out and about (both virtually and physically) she actively looks for like-minded local professionals to engage in conversation. Her Twitter conversation is a mixture of professional, for example her thoughts on marketing, and personal, such as her reactions to the weekend's big television show. Linkedin is Bryony's equivalent of her little black book. Every single person on her LinkedIn profile she has either worked with or met in a professional capacity.

Measuring your effectiveness

'Nobody gets paid for networking. We all get paid on the results of our networking.'

Rob Brown, motivational speaker and networking expert

❝You need to measure where you are having the most success❞ Successful networking takes time, money and effort. This means that you need to measure where you are having the most success with your networking efforts so you can replicate the things you are doing right and increase the effectiveness of your future results.

Look back to your networking goals which you set at the beginning of this chapter. How will you know when you are being successful? For example, if your prime aim is to secure a new job, you will know if you are being successful when you are talking with relevant companies and hiring managers who have a vacancy to fill.

What can you measure, and how regularly should you assess the effectiveness of your networking? For example you could measure:

■ the number of A-listers in your network where your relationship level is 3 or above

■ the number of people within your target market with whom you have a one-to-one conversation

■ the amount of business you receive via your network, and who the business comes from

■ the amount of help you receive from people within your network.

Let's look at a real-life example:

The networking goal: In April I set myself a goal to find a publisher, by October 31st via my network, for the book I wanted to write on networking.

The networking strategy: I had two main parts to my networking strategy:

1 Meet business book authors to gain introductions to their publishers.

2 Become known as an expert on networking so that a publisher would find me and ask me to write a book on networking for them.

The measurements of effectiveness I used:

■ Number of business book authors I meet, and progress the relationship to a Level 3.

■ Introductions to publishers.

■ Number of email and phone conversations with publishers.

■ Number of articles written on the subject of networking, which showcased me as an author of networking.

■ Number of reads of articles I had written on the subject of networking.

The result: Six weeks after setting my networking goal, I had gained four introductions to publishers, but was approached to write this book by Liz Gooster of Financial Times Prentice Hall. She had 'found' me by reading several of my articles on networking which I had posted on Business Zone.

Summary

There are six stages to building your networking strategy:

1 Set goals and objectives.

2 Identify who you need in your network.

3 Analyse the state of your current network.

4 Decide where you will meet the right people.

5 Decide how to measure your effectiveness.

6 Write your networking action plan (which we cover in the next chapter).

To be effective your network needs to contain people with whom you have a genuine connection, i.e. your relationship is at a minimum of Level 3, i.e. 'strengthen', 'collaborate' or 'inner circle'. For someone to be a genuine connection there needs to be trust present and they would happily recommend your services to others.

Finding the right place to network will take time and an element of experimentation. Constantly make adjustments to your strategy and plan as you grow and learn.

ACTION POINTS

■ Write a networking goal which will help you achieve personal, business and career success. Now demonstrate your commitment and hold yourself accountable by telling at least three people about your goal.

■ Who in your current network can help you achieve your networking goal – or introduce you to someone who can help you achieve your goal?

■ Write down everything you know about your ideal client and people well connected to them. What could you do to find out more about them?

■ Who do you know who may be a gatekeeper to your target market? How can you make contact with them and build a strong relationship?

■ Who do you know who is always introducing people and seems to know everyone? They may be a natural connector. How can you strengthen your relationship with them?

■ Tell three members of your family or friends about your business interests and ask them who they know who can help you.

■ Think about the A-listers within your network. For each A-lister analyse the state of the relationship. What level of relationship do you have with each of them? What do you need to do to strengthen the relationship?

■ Find three new places to network where you will meet your target market.

■ Thinking about your networking goal, what can you measure to determine how successful you are becoming?

Further resources

Books

The 29% Solution, Ivan Misner, PhD and Michelle R. Donovan, Olive Tree Press, 2008.

Eat That Frog! Get more of the important things done – today!, Brian Tracy, Berrett-Koehler Publishers, 2002.

The Tipping Point, Malcolm Gladwell, Abacus, 2001.

Websites

Joined Up Networking www.joinedupnetworking.com for worksheets to help you:

■ set your personal networking goals

■ identify your target client and A-lister

■ measure your networking success.

Rob Brown's blog www.rob-brown.com/Blog-Archive

14

Writing your joined up networking plan

What topics are covered in this chapter?

- How to use your networking opportunity score to focus your networking efforts
- What to do first to get started with online networking
- How to find the best local networking events
- How to choose the right social networking site for your networking strategy
- How to write a networking action plan

In the previous chapter we looked at the steps needed to build a successful joined up networking strategy. In this chapter we will focus on building a realistic plan to achieve your goals.

Using your networking opportunity score to focus your efforts

In Chapter 2 we identified four elements needed for a successful networking strategy: credibility, personal brand, visibility and social capital. While it may be impossible to predict where your next opportunity, e.g. job offer, new assignment, new client, speaking engagement, will come from, focusing on these four elements will help you to improve the likelihood of you generating opportunities via your network.

You will recall in Chapter 2, we linked these four elements by the following equation:

$$Opportunity = Credibility \times (Personal\ brand + Visibility + Social\ capital)$$

where

Opportunity represents an opportunity score. The greater this number, the higher the likelihood of opportunities coming to you.
Credibility = your personal credibility.

Table 14.1 Calculate your opportunity score

Score	Credibility The extent to which you deliver on your promises and 'walk your walk' and 'talk your talk'	Personal brand The marketability and strength of your personal brand
1	You have no track record in your specialist area, and are unlikely to write or talk about your specialist subject.	You are not distinguishable among your peers.
2	You may write or talk about your specialist subject. Some people ask your opinion, but often they are asking others ahead of you.	You are known among your close network as 'the person' who you need to talk to for 'y'.
3	You regularly write and talk about your specialist subject and are building up a small client list.	You have an active social media presence, and are known among your wide network as 'the person' who you need to talk to for 'y'.
4	You write and talk about your specialist subject regularly and have a well-stocked client list, with a few people using you as a trusted advisor.	You may have a book published, and have a very active social media presence – via blogging and social networking sites. Journalists will occasionally quote you. Your personal brand is now becoming stronger than your business's brand.
5	You are in constant demand to write and talk about your specialist subject. You have an impressive client list, and there are many people who use you as a trusted advisor.	You have written books, published articles, appeared on TV, presented at major conferences and are a household name within your industry or area of specialism.

Personal brand = the marketability and strength of your personal brand.

Visibility = visibility to your target market.

Social Capital = the amount of social capital you have generated within your network.

If you haven't already done so, thinking about your current networking goals, calculate your opportunity score using Table 14.1. Remember that there is no ideal score. Of course, the higher your score, the more likely it is that you will generate opportunities via your network. What Table 14.1

Visibility	*Social capital*
Your profile among your target market	*The influence and reach you have within your network*
Your target market has never heard of you.	Influential only among relatives and immediate work colleagues.
Your target market becomes aware of you.	Strong influence of up to 50 people.
Your name is known within your target market and you may have a small following on social media (< 1000 followers).	Strong influence of 51–150 people.
Your name is well known within your target market, and you are likely to have a medium-sized following (2000 followers or connections) on social media.	Strong influence of 151–500 people.
Your name is widely known within your target market, and are likely to have a large following (10,000 followers or connections) on social media.	Strong influence of 501+ people.

gives you is a way of focusing on activities which are the most likely to help you generate more opportunities from your networking activities.

Which of the four ingredients for a successful networking strategy do you need to spend time on to increase your likelihood of generating opportunities via your network? For example, if you are low on visibility, what do you need to do to increase your profile and top-of-the-mind visibility to your target audience?

You may like to brainstorm actions to improve your scores in each of the four areas (see Table 14.2). (This sheet is available as a downloadable worksheet on the joined up networking site: www.joinedupnetworking.com.)

What are three actions you could do to improve your opportunity score to help you achieve your networking goals? Write down these actions and set yourself a deadline to achieve them.

How to get started with online networking

❝Here is my eight-step quick guide to getting started❞

Over the past 12 months I've met many people who want to network online but don't know how to get started. If you are one of these people, here is my eight-step quick guide to getting started with online networking.

1 Write a short profile about youself, making sure you include relevant keywords within the description. (See Chapter 8 for how to write an online profile.)

This is my short profile, which I use as the basis for all the online profiles and biographies about me:

Heather Townsend is a widely published writer, social media expert and performance improvement specialist for professional services.

Heather in the last decade has worked with over one hundred partners, coaching and trained over 1000 lawyers, accountants and other professionals at every level, in the UK's top and most ambitious professional practices. She is the UK's foremost expert on how business people can build meaningful and profitable relationships via social media. She has been commissioned to write on key business topics by the *Financial Times*.

Heather is the co-founder of The Efficiency Coach and The Executive Village.

2 Then find a good-quality but low-resolution professional head-and-

Table 14.2 Brainstorming actions to improve your opportunity score

To increase my opportunity score, I could …

Credibility	Personal brand	Visibility	Social capital
■ Start a blog on my specialist subject	■ Start a blog on my specialist subject	■ Aim to meet at least one new person a week	■ Commit to following up with everyone I meet within 48 hours
■ Talk to my current clients to find out why they chose to work with me	■ Write my short online profile/bio	■ Spend an hour profiling and researching my ideal client	■ Join the committee of my professional association's local branch
■ Set up Google feed reader with blogs that are within my specialist area, and comment on one blog a week	■ Get a new professional photo taken of me	■ Ask my peers which events and groups they find helpful	■ Review the list of my A-listers and identify who I need to spend time with strengthening the relationship
■ Identify someone within my current company who I could work with on an assignment to increase my credibility	■ Speak to my colleagues and ask them what they believe that I stand for	■ Tag all my contacts in my address book as A, B or C-lister	
■ Find an online networking site where I can showcase my credentials		■ Commit to speaking to an A-lister at least once a week	
		■ Join a new networking group	

shoulders photo. It is worth having at least two professional photos available for you to use. For example, if you operate more than one Twitter account.

3   Join LinkedIn, Twitter, Facebook and a maximum of two other online forums.

4   Fill out your profile for the online networking sites which you have joined and follow the site's suggestions to connect with people you may already know on the site. For example, LinkedIn will go through your Microsoft Outlook and online address book to find people you already know on LinkedIn, and send a request to connect.

5   Start your own blog and write about a subject which showcases your credibility. Update your blog at least once a week. Use:

   ▪ The WordPress or Typepad application on LinkedIn to connect your blog to your LinkedIn profile

   ▪ Twitterfeed to connect your blog to your social networking status updates, e.g. Twitter and Facebook.

6   Introduce yourself to other people within your online networking sites.

7   Do a Google search for bloggers who write about subjects interesting to you, or subjects which match your specialism. Add the RSS feed from the blog into your RSS feed reader, for example Google Feed Reader.

8   Set aside a minimum of 30 minutes each day to go into your online networking sites and read the blogs in your Google Feed Reader. Aim to complete the following each day:

   ▪ A status update relevant to the audience on the site, for example keep your status updates on LinkedIn very professional, but light, personal and social on Facebook.

   ▪ A way of helping out someone on the site, for example answering a question or connecting two people together.

   ▪ Find up to five people every day to start a conversation with, whether this is commenting on a blog or chatting to someone on Twitter, answering a 'LinkedIn question' or joining in a discussion on an online forum.

   ▪ Share interesting content with your connections on your social networking sites.

How to find the best online networking sites

In Chapter 5 we identified all the different types of online networking sites available to the networker. With this amount of choice, it can be difficult to know where to spend your time online.

Before you can assess a site, you need to know what you want to achieve by maintaining a presence on that site. Or whether you want to maintain a visible presence at all – as there will be times when you have a very specific need. For example, there are many user forums available with a very specific goal, such as user forums for your satellite navigation system, or developer forums for a range of Wordpress themes. I have personally used these sites when I have a specific query rather than phoning customer services – and these sites are often removing the need for a front-line customer service function for a company.

Here are a few ideas to find the right online networking site for you:

- Do a Google search on 'online forum xxx', where xxx could be an industry, type of person or product which you need help with or want to meet.

- Have a look how many members are active on the site – you are looking for a minimum of 1000 members.

- Read the quality of the posts – is this a site which will enhance your credibility and personal brand by maintaining a regular presence?

- See how many of your competitors are regularly contributing to discussion threads. Too many of your peers may mean that the site is saturated with your particular specialism and it may take a while to build up a meaningful level of visibility and credibility.

- Ask questions on places like Twitter or LinkedIn to find online networking sites which other people rate.

How to find the best local networking events

Similar to finding the best online networking site to spend time on, there is no quick and easy answer to finding the best local networking events. One group or event may be perfect for one business or individual but ineffective for another. This is because people will always have personalised networking goals and networking preferences.

❝Never take someone else's word that a networking event or group is great❞ The best way to find potentially great local networking events is to ask around your network. Ideally, you want to find a group or event where you are made to feel welcome and given plenty of opportunities to get to know people. As you need to remember, effective networking is not about passing business, it's about building up relationships with people.

So you need to know what you are looking for – in terms both of your own networking objectives and also what makes a good, vibrant group. Never take someone else's word that a networking event or group is great – always visit a couple of times as a guest before committing to joining or attending regularly.

'Your decision to join a networking group should never be solely based on how nice the group is.'

Robert Watson, Managing Well

When you visit a group or event, take a temperature check on the atmosphere in the room.

■ Are there plenty of regulars?

■ Is the group knowledgeable and well connected?

■ Are there plenty of people who have been attending the group or event for a long time?

■ Is there energy and enthusiasm from the group or event's leader?

■ Are you made to feel welcome?

■ Do the regulars come up to talk to you?

■ Do people look as if they are having fun?

If you are attending a referral generation group, then also look out for the following signs:

■ What proportion of people are bringing referrals to the group?

■ Is the membership growing or declining?

How to effectively join up your networking activities

In my research for this book, I discovered that the most successful networkers don't see any distinction between online or face-to-face networking – it's all about choosing the right medium to connect with the right person.

There are two big hurdles for networkers when thinking about joining up their networking activities: fear of the unknown and knowing how to get started. There is a newer breed of networkers emerging who have grown up with Facebook and know how to naturally engage online, but struggle to work a room. Likewise there is the often older, skilled, face-to-face networker who is very comfortable with working a room and building rapport with others, but doesn't know where or how to start with online networking. As I have personally found out, there are greater rewards available to the networker who is prepared to embrace a joined up networking strategy.

To identify how you can effectively join up your networking activities, use the tools and processes worksheet (downloadable at Joined Up Networking, www.joinedupnetworking.com) to brainstorm ideas of how you can progress your contacts through the relationship levels. See Table 14.3 (overleaf) for an example.

Writing your networking action plan

It's time now to write your networking action plan. You may like to use our networking action plan worksheet to help you, which is downloadable at Joined Up Networking (www.joinedupnetworking.com).

Any networking action plan needs to contain the following items:

- Your networking goals and objectives.
- Your strategy – how you will achieve your networking goal.
- Your success criteria – how do you know when you are being successful with your networking?
- Your 'A-listers' and how will you meet them and stay in touch with them.
- An assessment of the networking 'assets' you have at the moment.

My networking goal:

- Find a new job as a learning and development specialist, within an hour's travel from home

My networking strategy: (who I need to meet to achieve my networking goal)

1. Meet Learning & Development directors, and HR directors of companies locally
2. Increase my network of UK-based HR professionals
3. Blog and tweet about leadership within professional services
4. Meet recruitment consultants specialising in placing learning and development professionals

Table 14.3 Progressing your contacts through the relationship levels

Relationship level	Online tools and processes	Face-to-face tools and processes
1: 'identify'	Twitter	Chamber of Commerce events
	Accounting Web	Inter-company socials
	LinkedIn Answers	
2: 'engage'	Follow and chat on Twitter	Email exchange
	Request to connect on LinkedIn	Send postcard to potential A-listers I meet
	Use questions in my blog posts	Join a mastermind group
	Answer questions on my blog post	
3: 'strengthen'	Exchange private messages on Twitter and LinkedIn	Phone call
	Connect on Skype	Skype video call
	Invite to connect on another social networking site	In-person meeting
4: 'collaborate'	Share blog links	Phone call
	LinkedIn closed group	Skype video call
		In-person meeting
		Join a small project team
5: 'inner circle'	Twitter – 'inner circle' list membership	Monthly meetings and diarised conversations
	Connect on personal Facebook page	

Who do I know already? (who could help me)	
Work colleagues (current or ex)	*Friends, family, neighbours*
1. My ex-boss Jo 2. My team	1. Next door neighbour works for NHS?
Old friends from school or college	*Suppliers, customers, clients*
1. Sarah 2. James	1. External trainers – Bridge
People I have met on training courses and at conferences	*People I know from non-work-related organisations I belong to*
	1. CIPD local branch committee
People in my address book	*Twitter followers, LinkedIn connections, Facebook friends or connections on other social networking sites*

Success criteria: (how do I know when I am being successful?)
1. I have increased the number of HR professionals I am connected to on LinkedIn from 15 to 300+ 2. I will be getting told about one new potential job every week 3. I will get an introduction to an HR or L&D director every month 4. I will have a new job, within an hour's travel of home, within 6 months

Current and future opportunities for networking	
Organisations I belong to	*Where do friends and colleagues network?*
1. CIPD local branch committee	1. Need to find out
Future conferences, training courses, project groups	*Online networking sites*

Who are my A-listers?	**Where or how to meet them?**	**How to stay in touch?**
Recruitment professionals	1. Ask for introductions via my current network 2. Look at job boards specialising in HR roles	1. Fortnightly phone call or email 2. Connect on LinkedIn 3. Follow on Twitter (if they tweet)

HR and learning & development directors, plus HR professionals generally	1. Attend CIPD events and conferences 2. Ask for introductions via my current network 3. Join LinkedIn groups with HR professionals 4. Answer LinkedIn questions on leadership 5. Blog at training zone and HR zone	1. Connect on LinkedIn 2. Comment on blogs about leadership issues 3. Link my blog to my LinkedIn profile and post in my LinkedIn groups 4. Ask for a phone call or meeting

Making yourself accountable

> **You need someone to keep you accountable to your goals**

For goals to be routinely achieved, you need someone to keep you accountable to your goals. If you are in employment this is very likely to be your line manager. If you are self-employed or looking for a new job, who can you use to keep you accountable to your networking action plan? Perhaps a partner, relative or good friend?

Summary

A plan turns your strategy into actions.

People's networking goals and preferences are very personal, and not every group, event or online networking site will suit everyone or be effective for everyone. Take the time to assess and research what are the best places for you personally to network to achieve your goal.

To harness the power of both face-to-face and online networking, decide which tools and processes you will use to strengthen the relationships which matter to you.

ACTION POINTS

■ Calculate your networking opportunity score. What are three actions you could do to improve your opportunity score to help you achieve your networking goals?

■ Find two different online networking sites which could help you meet potential A-listers.

▓ Look at your list of A-listers. Analyse the state of the relationship with each of them, and put in place an action plan to improve the level of the relationship with each of your A-listers.

▓ Ask two of your peers which, in their view, are the best local networking events and groups.

▓ Attend two new events or networking groups as a guest.

▓ Brainstorm tools and processes to strengthen relationships and maintain contact with your network. Make sure you include online and face-to-face tools and processes.

▓ Write your networking action plan, which will help you achieve your networking goal(s). Find someone to share your networking action plan with.

Further resources

Books

Never Eat Alone: And other secrets to success, one relationship at a time, 2nd edition, Keith Ferrazzi, Doubleday, 2011.

The 29% Solution, Ivan Misner, PhD and Michelle R. Donovan, Olive Tree Press, 2008.

Eat That Frog! Get more of the important things done – today! Brian Tracy, Berrett-Koehler Publishers, Inc, 2002.

Websites

Joined Up Networking www.joinedupnetworking.com for worksheets to help you:

▓ calculate your networking opportunity score

▓ brainstorm ways to increase your networking opportunity score

▓ identify tools and processes to strengthen the relationships in your network

▓ write your networking action plan.

15

How to fit it all in

What topics are covered in this chapter?

- Practical tips and techniques to be able to communicate with your network in a time-efficient manner

As you were reading through the book, I am sure you were thinking at various points, 'But how am I going to make the time to do all of this?' This chapter will show you how to use your networking time wisely and make your network work for you rather than the other way round.

Be realistic with your time

"You need to commit time to growing and maintaining your network"

Free time is the one thing that most busy professionals don't have. But to be successful at networking, you need to commit time to growing and maintaining your network. So, before you agree to attend lots of networking groups and maintain a highly visible presence on a range of online networking sites and tools, you need to be realistic about what time you have available for networking. For example, if you want to join a referral generation club and maximise your chances of generating referrals from club members, then you need to begin with the intention to have a one-to-one meeting with every single member of the club within the first couple of months of joining. Say, for example, the club has 20 members; once you include your travelling time and research, that's a minimum time commitment of 30+ hours. However, in reality you will be able to prioritise who you should meet first. If you join an online forum to generate business, you need to be prepared to visit and comment on that forum every single day.

As a general rule of thumb you want to be spending at least 50 per cent of your networking time maintaining and strengthening relationships within your current network.

Take a look at the vacant times in your diary – how much time do you realistically have to allocate to networking?

Experiment and measure results

A powerful networking strategy will always contain a mixture of ways to meet new people. As networking results are not a linear cause-and-effect relationship, not every group, event or forum will yield results you require. Over time you will find out that some groups, events and relationships have a better rate of return; potential A-listers will turn out to be C-listers, whereas a C-lister may turn out to be a useful B-lister or A-lister. (For a definition of what makes an A, B or C-lister see Chapter 7.) For example, I think of my next-door neighbour, who works for the local fire service, as a good friend, but in networking terms I class her as a C-lister. A week after I had told her that I was writing this book, she introduced me to someone who engaged me for some work. The moral of this story is to always leave open the communication channels between yourself and the C-listers within your network.

To make sure that you are investing your time in networking wisely, experiment with new groups and events, but regularly measure your results and progress so that you can see where or with whom to spend more time or less time to generate better results.

When you measure your results you can then fine-tune how much networking time you need to spend monthly to generate the level of results you require. For example, Bryony Thomas knows that she needs to physically meet ten people when networking each month to generate a healthy flow of new business.

Block out time in your diary

Follow-up and maintenance of a relationship takes time. The best way to efficiently follow up is to do what Karen Spillane does – she dedicates 30 minutes each day to following up and communicating with her network. Robert Watson, Executive Coach allocates two 30-minute periods each week, starting at 11:30 am, to follow up with his network. He chooses this time as it gives him a break from his morning work and helps him wind down to lunch. More importantly, Robert has found that many of his network are around at their desks and prepared to take a phone call at 11:30.

Block out time weekly and monthly in your diary to plan your networking time and activities. Use this time to prioritise who you need to meet and why.

Delegate

You can delegate some of your networking tasks to a personal or virtual assistant. For example, they can research:

■ people for you to meet

■ groups and events for you to attend

■ interesting content for you to write about or share.

As well as helping you with your research, they can take on some of the routine admin tasks, such as:

■ diary and meeting management

■ follow-up emails

■ entering contact details from business cards into your CRM software

■ running reports from your CRM software

■ posting your articles on blog sites.

Automate

❝ There are many tools available to the networker which help to save time ❞

Many networkers fall into the trap of thinking that they have to do everything themselves. There are many tools available to the networker which help to save time, such as the following.

Feed readers, such as Google Reader

Use these to 'read' all the important blogs and forum posts in one place.

Google Search Alerts

Use these to get alerted whenever content is created which contains a keyword which is important to you, such as your name.

Client relationship management software

This is a type of software which helps you manage your relationships and keep track of your conversations with your contacts. Some of these systems will allow you to connect with your contacts; social media profiles, so you can see all of your network's social media activity from one place. Most of these types of software will allow you to categorise all your contacts by adding tags. I recommend that you use the following tags to manage your network effectively:

Relationship level: 1 to 5
Importance to you: A, B or C-lister

With these tags you can run reports to help you prioritise who you need to spend time with. For example, you want to aim to have all your A-listers at a relationship level of 4 – 'collaborate' – or 5 – 'inner circle'.

Twitter and LinkedIn third-party applications

Use these often free pieces of software to use Twitter and LinkedIn more effectively. For example, there are applications which let you:

■ see just the tweets which matter to you, e.g. Tweetdeck and Hootsuite

■ link your Twitter, LinkedIn and blog, e.g. WordPress application for LinkedIn, Twitter application for LinkedIn

■ publish new posts from your blog to your social networking accounts, e.g. Twitterfeed

■ find people to follow and unfollow, e.g. Tweetspinner

■ find lists of people important to you

■ do keyword searches on Twitter

■ upload pictures and videos

■ and many other things.

Blog plugins

These are little pieces of coding which help you get more functionality from your blog. For example, these can:

■ connect your blog to Twitter

- optimise your blog for Google search engine rankings
- allow people to sign up for your newsletter from your blog
- stop spam comment protection
- and many other things.

Be discerning

Your time is precious, and networking takes time. Possibly the biggest time-wasting habit many networkers have is spending time meeting or maintaining relationships with the wrong type of people. Only you will know who you need to meet – however, it takes discipline and focus to leave a group, event or conversation which is not going to help you achieve your results. Get into the habit of routinely evaluating your conversations as you are having them – and always ask yourself, is this person or conversation going to help me achieve my goals? If the answer is 'no', then politely move on.

Spend time developing your networking skills

Networking, both face-to-face and online, is a skill which everyone can develop. Sadly, many professionals just jump in at the deep end when networking and don't take the time to attend any networking training, or even hone their networking skills by reading a book like this.

Do invest your time to undergo some personal development on networking. Far from being a sign of weakness, it is actually a sign that you are serious about your business and career success. Sometimes it's the small changes, such as how you introduce yourself, which actually have the biggest impact.

Look after your A-listers

'One good advocate is worth ten clients.'

Richard White, The Accidental Salesman® and Author of
The Accidental Salesman®: Networking survival guide[1]

Your A-listers are your word-of-mouth marketing team. These are your unpaid sales force. As they are 'unpaid', they have to *want* to recommend

---

[1] White, R., *The Accidental Salesman®: Networking survival guide*, Book Shaker, 2011.

❝Your A-listers are your word-of-mouth marketing team❞

you. Therefore, it is worth focusing your networking time on these people and looking after them as much as possible. Who can you introduce them to? How can you help them in their role? For example, one of my inner circle and A-listers is David Stoch, who runs Meerkat PR. He is very good at giving me a phone call fortnightly, in addition to the tweets we routinely exchange, to keep the relationship warm and mutually beneficial.

Network while you eat

Everyone needs to eat. When I was employed I used to use my lunch times to meet people in my network. Grabbing a coffee or a sandwich with someone you really want to meet can be an easy way to get a meeting with someone. How about inviting a few of your network for a meal? That way, they get to make new connections, you gain precious social capital, but more importantly you have been able to spend high-quality face-to-face time with several members of your network at the same time.

> **Tip**
>
> When meeting someone over lunch or dinner, order less than you normally would. This will allow you more time to talk and engage in conversation.

Do you need a face-to-face meeting?

When you add in travelling time, face-to-face meetings are a large investment from you. Before I will meet someone face-to-face I will normally have a phone or video-conference meeting with them. Only if, during this initial discussion, I see the potential for collaboration or a potential A-lister for me, will I then commit to a face-to-face meeting.

Keep the content on your online networking sites fresh

'The days when you would do a formal introduction on meeting someone new are now long gone. People have already checked you out on social media.'

Keith Robinson, www.careersiteadvisor.com

Get into the habit of regularly updating your status on your online networking sites. This is an easy and quick way of keeping in touch with many of your network at once. Often I find that my status updates will prompt a conversation with one of my network.

Summary

Allocate time each week to networking. Put in place a process or system to help you maintain contact with your existing A-listers. Then spend some time finding and meeting up with new A-listers.

Wherever possible, delegate or automate the admin tasks to free up your time.

ACTION POINTS

■ Plan 30 minutes a day in your diary to help you keep in contact with your network.

■ Identify three tasks to help you maintain your network which you could delegate or automate.

■ Next time you are in an unproductive conversation at a networking event, have a go at politely withdrawing from the conversation.

■ Think who you could ask to join you for lunch next week. Now go and book your lunch date.

■ Plan a networking lunch or dinner with three other people within your network who you think would benefit from knowing each other.

■ Find three different ways in which you could help A-listers within your network this week.

■ Commit to updating your Facebook and LinkedIn status every day for a month. Notice how many more conversations this prompts with your network.

Further resources

Books

The 7 Habits of Highly Effective People, Stephen Covey, Simon & Schuster, 2004.

Never Eat Alone: And other secrets to success, one relationship at a time, 2nd edition, Keith Ferrazzi, Doubleday, 2011.

Websites

Joined Up Networking www.joinedupnetworking.com

My personal efficiency blog http://personal-efficiency.theefficiencycoach.co.uk

16

A final word about networking

The relentless pace of developments in communications technology is rapidly changing how people interact across geographical and cultural boundaries. It's pretty much a given, in this internet-enabled age, that future success will come easily to those savvy professionals who have worked out who they need to know *and* how to easily get found by others. For these professionals, their network has become intrinsic to their current and future business success. It's this network which will provide them with the answers, guidance and opportunities needed to get ahead in business.

If you want to be one of those savvy professionals, it all comes down to proactively answering and acting on the answers to these three simple questions about your network:

- Who do you need to add into your network?
- Where to meet them?
- How to maintain and strengthen the relationships?

❝No employer or competitor can ever take your network away from you❞

Your network is your own, and something that will accompany you as you go through life. No employer or competitor can ever take your network away from you. It's a personal asset which, if invested in, will yield a rate of return far greater than any other form of activity, process or system.

Whether you realise it or not, you are networking every time you start a conversation. You have a choice – how will you use those conversations?

Will you actively look to build relationships with people in a position to help you generate career and business success?

Or will you carry on as before…?

Glossary

4N or 4Networking a UK-based networking organisation which has groups which meet all over the UK, as well as an active online forum.

40 or 60 second pitch another name for the short pitch which many networking groups require each member to deliver each time they meet.

A-lister someone who is well connected to your target market and an advocate for your services.

App a piece of software commonly found on smart phones which is used to give additional functionality to the hardware device.

Athena a women-only networking group.

Avatar the picture which online networking sites displays of their members.

Bing Microsoft's search engine.

Blog or weblog An online journal based on the web.

Blogger someone who hosts or writes a blog, as well as a popular piece of blogging software.

Blogging the practice of writing a blog.

Blogosphere a term used to describe blogs on the internet.

BNI the largest referral generation organisation in the world. Most referral generation clubs are based on BNI in some way.

Business card a small, wallet-sized piece of card with a person's contact details on.

Business for Breakfast or B4B a franchise-based referral generation club in the UK.

Conversation thread the continuing conversation or discussion on an internet forum.

CPD points some professional institutes require their members to record and complete a certain number of continuing professional development hours or points.

Credibility your ability to walk your walk, talk your talk, and deliver on your commitments.

DM shorthand for direct message – a way of sending private messages between users on Twitter.

Drupal blogging software.

Elevator pitch term used for the short sales pitch which networkers are often asked to deliver at networking events.

Facebook the largest social network in the world.

Feedburner a service provided by Google, which allows people to easily subscribe to your blog in a medium, e.g. via RSS or email, which suits them.

Flaming the act of inciting an argument on a social networking site.

Google the world's most popular search engine.

Guest speaker many networking events use a guest speaker as a focal point of the event.

Hiring manager the individual in a company or organisation responsible for hiring a new member of staff.

Jelly groups groups where freelancers and self-employed people meet up to work together.

Joined up networking the practice of using both online and face-to-face networking for greater business and career success.

Lead a potential enquiry or opportunity to gain business.

LinkedIn a social networking site frequented by professionals. It has been likened to the professional's version of Facebook.

LinkedIn Answers a part of LinkedIn where users ask questions to the users on LinkedIn.

LinkedIn groups private and public communities on LinkedIn.

Mastermind group a group of people who meet regularly to give each other peer-to-peer mentoring and support.

Micro-blogging a form of blogging where users are limited to only being able to post short messages. Twitter is probably the best known form of micro-blogging.

Monthly minute another name for an elevator pitch.

My Space social networking site focused around music.

Ning a piece of software which allows people to have their own social networking site.

Non-executive or non-exec experience a mastermind group.

Online forums websites where registered users can post up discussions or contribute to discussions by replying to the original post.

Online networking the practice of meeting people via the internet.

Online profile or biography an introduction to you which most online networking sites ask every user to fill out.

OP or original poster the person who starts a discussion on an online forum.

Page rank a weighting Google gives each website which determines how frequently it returns to each site to see if any content has changed. The higher the page rank, the more visits from Google.

Peeps or tweeters what people on Twitter call themselves.

Personal branding what people say about you when you are out of the room.

Plaxo an online address book site.

Plugin a piece of coding which 'plugs' into a piece of software to give it additional functionality. Used extensively with open source software, such as WordPress.

PM shorthand for a private message on a social networking site.

Post an entry in a online forum or blog.

Posterous free blogging software.

Profession lock-out policy the practice of allowing only one type of a certain profession in a networking group, e.g. only one accountant is allowed within the group.

Referral when one of your network passes you an opportunity.

Referral generation group or club a group of people who have joined together to help each other generate referrals for the wider group.

Retweet or RT when people on Twitter share someone's tweet with all their followers.

RSS (Really Simple Syndication) feed a way of easily updating people interested in your site when it changes.

RSS reader a piece of software which allows you to read RSS feeds in one place. Google Reader is a type of RSS reader.

Skype™ a service which allows users to make free video or audio calls over the internet to other Skype™ users.

Slideshare a site where users can share their presentations.

Smart phone a phone which (as well as taking phone calls) can access the internet.

SMS the service normally used to send text messages or text-based chat conversations.

Social bookmarking a type of social networking site where users on the site share bookmarks to websites.

Social capital the imaginary emotional bank account that you build up by being helpful to people.

Social media a collection of data, photos and video assembled by users.

Social networking websites which allow users to group together in communities.

Spammer someone who sends you unsolicited messages for their products.

Speed networking a form of networking where participants have a short, timed conversation before moving on to talk to someone else at the event.

Status updates functionality on a social networking site which allows users to post up messages about their status.

Sub short for substitute. Members at a referral group are often required to send a substitute if they cannot attend a meeting.

Teleseminar a form of seminar where participants join in over the telephone.

Troll a term for someone who deliberately posts up negative or highly critical comments, blogs or posts.

Tweet a message on Twitter, which is limited to 140 characters.

Tweeters what people on Twitter call themselves.

Tweeting the practice of using Twitter to send messages.

Twitter a micro-blogging service which limits users to posts of a maximum of 140 characters.

Twitter lists a function on Twitter where users can group together followers.

Twitterati highly influential and often visible users of Twitter.

URL the address of a web page.

URL shortening service a service which allows you to shorten addresses of web pages – vital if you are limited only to 140 characters in your updates.

User profiles information about you entered into a social networking site.

Virtual boardroom a mastermind group.

VOIP telephony services which are provided over the internet. Perhaps the best known VOIP service is Skype™.

Webinar a form of seminar where listeners join in over the web.

Weblog the first name and form of blogs.

WiBN shorthand for the Women in Business Network.

WordPress an open source piece of blogging software.

Working the room a phrase which describes the practice of finding people to talk to in a room full of strangers.

Xing a social networking site.

Yahoo a search engine, email provider and news site.

Yammer a private micro-blogging site. An 'in-house' version of Twitter.

YouTube a video-sharing site, and the second biggest search engine after Google.

Further resources

Books

Networking and relationship building

Brilliant Networking: What the best networkers, know, do and say, 2nd edition, Stephen D'Souza, Prentice Hall, 2010.

Recommended: The ultimate masterclass in selling through referrals and networking, Andy Lopata, Financial Times Prentice Hall, 2011.

Confident Networking for Career Success and Satisfaction, Gael Lindenfield and Stuart Lindenfield, Piatkus Books, 2005.

Networking Like A Pro: Turning contacts into connections, Ivan R. Misner, David C. Alexander and Brian Hilliard, Entrepreneur Press, 2010.

The 29% Solution, Ivan Misner, PhD and Michelle R. Donovan, Olive Tree Press, 2008.

Never Eat Alone: And other secrets to success, one relationship at a time, 2nd edition, Keith Ferrazzi, Doubleday, 2011.

Get Off Your Arse, Brad Burton, 4Publishing, 2009.

Professional Networking for Dummies, Donna Fisher, John Wiley & Sons, 2001.

Perfect Phrases for Professional Networking, Susan Benjamin, McGraw-Hill Professional, 2009.

Nice Girls Don't Get the Corner Office, Lois Frankel, Little, Brown & Company, 2004.

*The Accidental Salesman®: Networking survival guide – the essential hands-on manual for winning more business and gaining new sales lead*s, Richard White, Book Shaker, 2011.

The Jelly Effect: How to make your communications stick, Andy Bounds, Capstone, 2010.

… And Death Came Third! The definitive guide to networking and speaking in public, Andy Lopata and Peter Roper, Book Shaker, 2006.

What Color Is Your Parachute? Richard Nelson Bolles, Ten Speed Press, 2008.

Eat That Frog! Get more of the important things done – today! Brian Tracy, Berrett-Koehler Publishers, 2002.

The 7 Habits of Highly Effective People, Stephen Covey, Simon & Schuster, 2004.

Social media and online networking

This Is Social Media: Blog, tweet, link your way to business success, Guy Clapperton, Capstone, 2009.

Socialnomics: How social media transforms the way we live and do business, 2nd edition, Erik Qualman, John Wiley & Sons, 2010.

Social Media 101: Tactics and tips to develop your business online, Chris Brogan, John Wiley & Sons, 2010.

Inbound Marketing: Get found using Google, social media and blogs, Brian Halligan and Dharmesh Shah, John Wiley & Sons, 2009.

Get up to Speed with Online Marketing: How to use websites, blogs, social networking and much more, Jon Reed, Financial Times Prentice Hall, 2010.

Trust Agents: Using the web to build influence, improve reputation and earn trust, revised edition, Chris Brogan and Julien Smith, John Wiley & Sons, 2010.

Blogging

WordPress for Business Bloggers, Paul Thewlis, Packt Publishing, 2008.

ProBlogger: Secrets for blogging your way to a six-figure income, 2nd edition, Darren Rowse and Chris Garrett, John Wiley & Sons, 2010.

Building an online community

Managing Online Forums, Patrick O'Keefe, Amacom, 2008.

Groundswell, Josh Bernoff and Charlene Li, Harvard Business School Press, 2008.

Personal branding

Me 2.0: Build a powerful brand to achieve career success, revised edition, Dan Schawbel, Kaplan Trade, 2010.

Social capital

Influence: The psychology of persuasion, revised edition, Robert Cialdini, 1st Collins Business Essentials, 2007.

The Tipping Point, Malcolm Gladwell, Abacus, 2001.

Cultural diversity

Kiss, Bow or Shake Hands, Terri Morrison and Wayne A. Conaway, Adams Media Corporation, 2006.

Riding the Waves of Culture: Understanding cultural diversity in business, Fons Trompenaars and Charles Hampden-Turner, Nicholas Brealey Publishing, 1997.

Websites and blogs

Business networking

Joined Up Business Networking for Professionals http://joinedupnetworking.com

Dan Schawbel's Personal Branding blog www.personalbrandingblog.com

Ivan Misner's Networking Now blog http://businessnetworking.com

Andy Lopata's Connecting is not enough blog www.lopata.co.uk/blog

Rob Brown's blog www.rob-brown.com/Blog-Archive

Melissa Kidd's Blog www.melissakidd.co.uk

Keith Ferrazzi's blog on relationship building www.keithferrazzi.com

Online networking

Just professionals www.justprofessionals.net

Joined Up Business Networking for Professionals http://joinedupnetworking.com

Social media

Chris Brogan's blog www.chrisbrogan.com

Mashable http://mashable.com

Cultural diversity

Executive Planet www.executiveplanet.com

Kwintessential www.kwintessential.co.uk/resources/country-profiles.html

Cyborlink www.cyborlink.com

Blogging software

WordPress http://wordpress.org and http://wordpress.com

Drupal www.drupal.org

Blogger www.blogger.com

Posterous www.posterous.com

Online community hosting

Yahoo groups http://uk.groups.yahoo.com

LinkedIn groups www.linkedin.com/directory/groups

Facebook groups www.facebook.com/groups

Facebook business and community pages www.facebook.com/pages/create.php?

Ning www.ning.com

Buddypress www.buddypress.org

SocialGO www.socialgo.com

Downloadable worksheets and templates from Joined Up Business Networking – www.joinedupnetworking.com

- Client analysis worksheet
- Opportunity score brainstorm worksheet
- Online profile template
- Elevator/60 second pitch template
- Networking tools and processes worksheet
- Networking action plan
- Guide to personal branding

Names and contact details of UK-based networking organisations

Referral generation groups

BNI www.bni.com

4Networking www.4networking.biz

Business for Breakfast www.bforb.com

NRG www.nrg-networks.com

Viva Business Networking www.viva-networking.co.uk

Netlinked www.netlinked.co.uk

Mix-and-mingle events

Local Chambers of Commerce www.britishchambers.org.uk

The Federation of Small Businesses www.fsb.org.uk

Institute of Directors www.iod.com

The Best Of www.thebestof.co.uk

Mastermind groups

The Executive Village www.executivevillage.co.uk

Vistage's executive peer groups www.vistage.co.uk

Academy for Chief Executives www.chiefexecutive.com

Inspired Mastermind Groups www.theinspiredgroup.com

Refer On www.refer-on.com

Women-only networking groups

Athena http://theathenanetwork.com

Women in Business Network www.wibn.co.uk

WiRE (Women in Rural Enterprise) www.wireuk.org

Women's business clubs www.thewomensbusinessclubs.com

Parent-friendly networking groups

Mum's the Boss www.mumstheboss.co.uk

Mum's Business Club mumsbusinessclub.com

Social networking sites

Site	URL	Notes
Facebook	www.facebook.com	Largest social networking site in the world
LinkedIn	www.linkedin.com	Facebook for 'professionals'
Twitter	www.twitter.com	Micro-blogging site

The Executive Village	www.executivevillage.co.uk	Mainly UK business owners and senior decision makers
Ecademy	www.ecademy.com	Business owners from all over the world
Xing	www.xing.com	Similar to LinkedIn with a large European community
Plaxo	www.plaxo.com	Online address book
UK Business Forums	www.ukbusinessforums.co.uk	Mainly UK SME business owners, but a good international presence
UK Business Labs	www.ukbusinesslabs.co.uk	Mainly UK-based SME business owners
Everywoman UK	www.everywoman.com	Female entrepreneurs, mainly UK based
Startupnation	www.startupnation.com	Community of start-up business owners
The small business community forums	www.smallbusinessforums.org	Community for small business owners

Index